D0285619

"Few life-travelers have earned the right to teac... us more than Shelly Miller. This kind of stellar writing cannot be faked. My book recommendation stack has grown smaller through the years, but this one is now on the list."

—Lisa Whittle, author of *Jesus Over Everything*, speaker, and podcast host

"At our core, we all long to belong. Somewhere along the way uncertainty causes us to question everything. In *Searching for Certainty*, Shelly arrives as a trusted guide and companion for such a time as this, reminding us of our worth and to whom we eternally belong."

—Kristin Schell, founder of The Turquoise Table

"Shelly's words come from a deep-forged well. Because of where she's been and her reach for God from that place, her words lead . . . and they heal. We need more writers, life-framers, like Shelly."

—Sara E. Hagerty, bestselling author of *Every Bitter Thing Is Sweet*, *Unseen*, and *Adore*

"Shelly Miller couldn't have known how timely her book would be, but that is only proof of her message: We don't need certainty of circumstance to live faithful, fruitful lives. This book is personal, poetic, and practical. Beautifully shaped by Shelly's gift for photography and storytelling, it is a book for every uncertain season of our lives."

—Christie Purifoy, author of *Placemaker* and cohost of the Out of the Ordinary podcast

"A lot of people write books, but not many live those books like Shelly. Her words leak with a presence of someone full of wisdom and love—someone who has lived a life we want to glean everything from! We are so grateful for her and this book, and we know you will be too."

—Jefferson and Alyssa Bethke, cofounders of familyteams.com and authors of *Love That Lasts*

"*Searching for Certainty* is a refreshing voice for struggling hearts. For those desperate for Christ's presence in unstable times, every page is compassionately truthful, vividly relevant, and readily applicable to the uncertain seasons of our lives."

—Phylicia Masonheimer, national bestselling author

"Shelly has taken me on a journey that has inspired me. Her deep sympathy for personal struggles in life has left me with a deep feeling of hope and certainty of God's love. This book is a treasure."

—Sally Clarkson, director, Sallyclarkson.com

"Shelly's words continue to mentor me. In *Searching for Certainty*, you'll be challenged and encouraged by a thought leader, beauty hunter, and profound question-asker. I look forward to referring back to this book many times for the rest of my life."

—Myquillyn Smith, *Wall Street Journal* bestselling author of *Cozy Minimalist Home*

Searching

FOR

Certainty

Searching

FOR

Certainty

FINDING GOD
IN THE
DISRUPTIONS
OF LIFE

SHELLY MILLER

BETHANYHOUSE
a division of Baker Publishing Group
Minneapolis, Minnesota

Published by Bethany House Publishers
11400 Hampshire Avenue South
Bloomington, Minnesota 55438
www.bethanyhouse.com

Bethany House Publishers is a division of
Baker Publishing Group, Grand Rapids, Michigan

Printed in the United States of America

Library of Congress Control Number: 2020941810

ISBN 978-0-7642-3597-9 (paperback)
ISBN 978-0-7642-3828-4 (casebound)

This book recounts events in the life of Shelly Miller according to the author's recollection and from the author's perspective. While all the stories are true, some dialogue and identifying details have been changed to protect the privacy of the people involved.

Cover design by Rob Williams, InsideOut Creative Arts
Poetry and interior photos by Shelly Miller

Published in association with Books & Such Literary Management, www.booksandsuch.com

20 21 22 23 24 25 26   7 6 5 4 3 2 1

For my children,
Murielle and Harrison.
May the certainty of God's love
be your constant companion.

CONTENTS

FOREWORD

YOU DECIDE TO buy a certain kind of car, and suddenly you see it everywhere. A friend recommends an obscure movie to you, and by the end of the week, three more people have mentioned it. You find out you're having a baby and now you're surrounded by pregnant women in every shopping aisle, church classroom, and train station. It's not just you, and it is a real thing. So real, in fact, that there are actual names for it. Known as Blue Car syndrome, or the Baader-Meinhof phenomenon, this is when we hear or experience something and suddenly it seems to appear everywhere. It's also called *frequency illusion*, which, of course, implies these things are not, in actuality, happening or appearing more often than normal, but because they have been brought to your attention, your brain notices them more often.

For the last four years, I've been paying close attention to what happens around me and within me when I have a decision to make. Once my brain was tuned in to this, I saw the impact of unmade decisions everywhere I looked. I noticed how unmade decisions hold a lot of power, and most of us fall into one of two categories: decisive or indecisive. For the decisive ones among us, unmade decisions are not allowed to linger. They demand attention and are quickly given direction. But not everyone makes decisions swiftly.

For the rest of us, unmade decisions often lead to chronic hesitation and a long process of research, consideration, and even procrastination until we get assurance that we're headed in the right direction. It doesn't matter if the decision is a small one, like which color to paint the kitchen, or a larger one, like which job offer to accept. We are afraid to choose wrong, overwhelmed by the number of options, and ultimately unsure we have what it takes to hear God's voice. The unmade decision becomes our highest priority and we begin to look everywhere for clues to an answer. To sum it up, we are *searching for certainty*.

In my continued fascination with the decision-making process, one thing I've noticed is how God seems less concerned with the decisions we make and more concerned with the way we make decisions. The focus is less on what we do and more on *who we are*. And that is one of the many reasons I've fallen in love with this book. It reads as an anthem for the chronically hesitant among us, gently guiding us away from the belief that this life is up to us, inviting us instead to enter into the larger story of God. Through sharing her personal story and her honest faith, Shelly Miller shows us God's heart toward us when we have questions, objections, and doubt. Yes, we may be walking in the dark, but God is with us. Yes, we may be carrying questions, but God sees us. Yes, we may not know what comes next, but the Lord is near. And maybe we need this message now more than ever before.

On December 31, 2019, my husband and I rang in the New Year with a few friends, our kids, a toast, some laughter, and snacks shared around our scuffed-up kitchen table. The simplicity of those moments stands in stark contrast to the complexity of what the world has had to face in 2020. We didn't know as we crossed the invisible threshold into a new decade that we had just welcomed in the year that would perhaps become the most uncertain the modern world has yet to see, forced to navigate the impact of a global pandemic. It's fair to say if we weren't familiar with uncertainty before, this year changed that. It may not be what we expected and certainly not what we wanted, but nevertheless, here we are, a global community, facing the most uncertain days of our generation.

In these pages, Shelly's words read like those from a woman who could see the future. How did she know we would need this book at this exact time in history? How could her personal story so parallel our communal one? How could her words be so perfectly timed, poured together in a recipe of hope for such a time as this? Of course, Shelly didn't know, but our friend Jesus knew, and he offers us comfort through the words of his daughter. I've never been more grateful for the timing of a book. As Shelly's story unfolds, watch her *become someone* not in spite of uncertainty but perhaps because of it. And as we bear witness to her becoming, may it be so in us as well.

Emily P. Freeman, author of The Next Right Thing

"Our hunger is the exile's hunger, but it is also the first step in our homecoming. We hunger, and in doing so learn the shape of our emptiness is the world's great emptiness in or to prepare room for God's presence. We imagine we are cultivating good or friendship or beauty. But we are, in all of these ways, cultivating God's glory in our midst."

—Christie Purifoy, *Roots and Sky*

ONE

Reframing Uncertainty

It flames from within,
unseen yet never dims

In wind, storm, or gale
it flickers with your exhale

So close, my Father's breath,
so intimate, his warmth

To live is to breathe shining

MAKE A WISH! It's what every child hears as they inhale before
blowing out flaming candles on a birthday cake, marking another year. I wished my life were different almost every day of
my childhood. A yellowing picture from a sparse collection of
childhood photos hangs above my writing desk, a reminder that
my life began clouded by uncertainty. In celebration of my third
birthday, I'm bent over a white frosted cake embellished with
flaming candles, one pink, one blue, and one of an indiscernible
color. The photo illustrates an ephemeral frame of my story, lived

but not remembered, and often retold by relatives as *the year Shelly didn't smile.* My third year of stoic quietness accompanies a hunger strike coinciding with my parents' decision to end their short union. Age and experience aren't requirements for the soul to know something is awry, slanting the natural order of things. Searching for certainty is foundational to our DNA.

Of English descent, Dad and I share the thin bridge of our nose becoming a bright shade of pink when we stand in the sunny outdoors longer than fifteen minutes. Even with belts around our waists, we each maintain the habit of pulling up our pants due to small hips. His wavy brown hair and thin lips are my inheritance, but the twinkle in those marble blues when he smiles, well, those eyes set him apart as my grandfather's son. Being Dave's daughter sounds magical when I hear other people say it out loud.

Dad was twenty-four, on the verge of completing his junior year of law school, when he pursued my mother, an attractive reservation agent with Trans World Airlines (TWA), who preferred wearing Saks Fifth Avenue from head to toe. A few months into their relationship, he received the untimely news of her suspected pregnancy. One academic year away from receiving a diploma, embarking upon a career and claiming independence, the last thing he envisioned was becoming a husband and a parent. But raised as a staunch Catholic by two devout parents, he followed conviction over scruples, choosing marriage at the semester break to give my life legitimacy. But the pregnancy was kept a secret from both sides of the family until I entered the world on the ninth of August at St. Joseph Hospital in St. Louis, Missouri. Once the math was calculated by unsuspecting relatives, my parents' secret was revealed and the weight of judgment was released onto Dad's shoulders. He would never practice law, but the secret he defended was the single case that haunted him for rest of his life. Did he do the right thing? Did he plead the case well before the court of disapproving witnesses? What could he have done differently?

From their fractured beginning, the marriage between my mother and father was anything but good. *Not enough* was the mantra heard repeatedly, especially when it came to money. Searching for the certainty of her happiness, Dad borrowed money from his parsimonious father for a down payment on a newly constructed condo, hoping to create some security in his marriage. They moved in and settled down, but a short time later, upon arriving home from a business trip in Georgia, he opened the door to an empty house. The only evidence of their union left behind was a framed picture of his bride on their wedding day, hanging on a blank wall. Mom filed for divorce and Dad resumed living with his parents.

During their separation, home for me was with Dad. We developed a Wednesday rhythm of picking up carryout at a local fast-food restaurant, enjoying time together while Grandma and Grandpa were out on a routine dinner date. Decades later, when Dad informs me that my favorite childhood meal was a cheeseburger, mashed potatoes, and milk shake, those seemingly random details become a revelation, bringing new insight to old cravings: frequenting the Dairy Queen drive-thru for dip cones while pregnant with my firstborn, Murielle, and the McDonald's drive-thru for cheeseburgers during the nine months I carried my son, Harrison. Who you are at the core arises as revelation amid major markers shaping your life.

Divorce in the 1960s was an era when courts granted full custody more often to women. By the time I blew the candles out on that frosted homemade cake in the photograph, my parents' divorce was final and home transitioned to living with Mom. As stipulated by the court, time with Dad was limited to weekends. Our Wednesday dinner dates ended, and a short time later, I declared a hunger strike.

To create some stability again, my parents agreed that I should return to the security of my grandparents' house, living temporarily in the company of Dad. But I still refused to eat anything. In desperation, Dad drove back to the little hamburger joint, ordered a milk shake, carried it home, placed the sweet, creamy drink in front of me, and much to his delight, watched the contents slowly disappear. For two weeks, daily sustenance came in the form of a milk shake slurped through a straw. Then one evening, he departed from the safety of the familiar, bringing home an order of mashed potatoes to accompany my liquid diet. "I remember being so excited to tell my parents about your eating the potatoes when they got home," Dad writes to me in an email.

For several weeks, mashed potatoes and milk shakes were manna provided by my father until slowly, steadily, I began departing from the familiar to try new food. Dad delivers the good report to Mom and I return to her house the next day. One week later, she calls with more dire news: I am refusing to eat again. And Dad starts the process all over again.

Before my father filled in the cracks of my foundations, I memorized that old photograph of myself and discerned a different narrative based on my adult expression at three years of life: Unhappy and unloved, I was an unwanted intrusion into my parents' lives. It wasn't until I boldly asked, decades later, about the details of how my life began that I gained understanding and empathy. When I look at that picture now, my sober expression translates as discernment and self-protection with a large dose of stubbornness. Early on, life was out of sorts, and I chose to turn inward as a result of worry, a first response to uncertainty. With self-awareness that comes by way of maturity and life experiences, I translate my refusal to smile as *I'm not going to give you what you want* (a smile for the photo) *if I can't trust you to give me what I need* (security). You could say I've been searching for the certainty of proof that I am worthy of love ever since I blew the candles out on that cake.

And aren't we all on a similar pilgrimage—looking for proof that we are worthy of love and belonging when the circumstances of life make us feel like exiles? When a career is replaced by a bot, a church splits due to irreconcilable differences over theology, a friendship dissolves in betrayal, and livelihood is compromised by a health diagnosis, self-protection is our knee-jerk reaction. It is human nature to turn inward, self-reflect, and assess current uncertainty through the lens of our circumstances. But God requires something different from us. Look up and make eye contact with him amid the disruptions of life.

Exiled from his own people, perhaps Moses was looking for proof that he was worthy of love and belonging too, as he watched an Egyptian beat up a Hebrew, a man who could've been his distant relative. What provoked him to watch his people endure the ravages of hard labor? What question might he have been trying to answer? What false narrative had he made into truth? Moses chose murder over love. How might his actions been different had he chosen to look up rather than out?

> Early on, life was out of sorts, and I chose to turn *inward* as a result of worry, a first response to *uncertainty*.

Because God was watching the Hebrews too. But his response was compassion and liberation, freedom from captivity. Ironically, God chose Moses to lead his own people into freedom, a man prone toward self-reliance rather than relying on God. They watched. Both Moses and God were watching the same people from different perspectives. The Egyptians could've been wiped out in a breath, but God offered the choice of response first. What are you watching? How are you making assessments of the world? How might looking up reorient your perspective back to hope?

Not enough was the cry of the Israelites in response to the fear of uncertainty threaded throughout the Exodus story. *I am not enough* was Moses' knee-jerk reaction to God's request from a burning bush to lead the Israelites out of captivity. *Not enough* is ultimately our deepest fear when we encounter the wilderness of the unknown as we journey through life. Maybe right now, as you hold this book in your hands, you fear that you won't have enough time, food, money, influence, approval, friendships, support—you fill in the blank. What is missing in your life that God is *not enough* for you? What situations are you attempting to solve with self-reliance instead of reliance on God?

The unknown scares me. Uncertainty creates resistance. I like to visualize the lay of the land before taking a leap into new territory. And if all is unfamiliar and I don't have a clue, I tend to self-protect and turn inward. Protect the familiar like it's my job and then wrestle through perfectionism until I finally surrender to risk.

When impossible situations interrupt the hopeful future we envision, we are prone to revert to the familiar as comfort, even when we know the familiar might not be God's best for us. A glass of wine to numb stress, quick social media scrolls to feel less alone, a shopping spree to perk up sadness, binge-watching Netflix as an escape from disappointment, the taste of a chocolate milk shake to fill the deep void of grief.

Three days after God provides a miracle in parting the Red Sea, ushering the Israelites into safety, that miracle in moments of desperation becomes a faded memento forgotten once stomachs begin growling. In the desert, it was as if the whole community had amnesia when their hunger was unsatiated. "If only we had died by the LORD's hand in Egypt! There we sat around pots of meat and ate all the food we wanted, but you have brought us out into this desert to starve this entire assembly to death" (Exodus 16:3).

It is scary to open one's self to the dark of the divine, giving up control that brings an illusion of safety with it. Mystery can make you hesitant to hope, decidedly prone toward doubt, and more anxious for preferred outcomes. *Who am I? Why me? Why now?* Those were the first questions Moses asked when God tasked him with leading the Israelites out of slavery and into freedom. And they are the same questions that haunt us when uncertainty flares like a burning bush on the sidewalks of suburban life.

ACCORDING TO THE World Health Organization, one in thirteen globally suffers from anxiety. In the United States, one in five adults have a mental health condition. That's over forty million Americans; more than the populations of New York and Florida combined. Depression is the leading cause of disability worldwide. Almost 75 percent of people with mental disorders remain untreated in developing countries, with almost one million people taking their lives each year. Studies also reveal that loneliness has become an epidemic affecting over half the population in the United States. Those numbers are staggering.[1]

In the *Independent*, Alex Williams writes, "Anxiety is starting to seem like a sociological condition, too: a shared cultural experience that feeds on alarmist CNN graphics and metastasizes through social media.

"As depression was to the 1990s . . . so it seems we have entered a new Age of Anxiety. Monitoring our heart rates. Swiping ceaselessly at our iPhones. Filling meditation studios in an effort to calm our racing thoughts. Consider the fidget spinner: endlessly whirring between the fingertips of Generation Alpha, annoying teachers and baffling parents."[2]

Wars, pandemics, recessions, technological changes, work/life alterations—all contribute to a massive cultural transition taking place around the globe. Whom can I trust? Where do I belong? What will my future hold? Does anyone truly care about me? How can I find peace amid transition? These are the questions that haunt all of us in today's busy world. And they were the same questions heard from the Israelites as they wandered through the desert with Moses thousands of years ago.

Transitioning from the familiarity of captivity to the unknowns of the desert, the exiles were unsure if God was going to make good on his promises. Are we loved or are we damned? Will the Promised Land be worth the long, arduous journey rife with uncertainty? Or will adversity and hardship divert the Israelites from the good God has planned for them? Spoiler alert: There *is* a happy ending. But happy endings don't often come without navigating times of uncertainty first.

Read the story of the Exodus and you may be skeptical about God's promises still being relevant for you today. Will adversity that comes by way of racism, sexism, violence, terrorism, plagues, and politics keep us from the good God has planned in the future? Can you trust that where God is leading you is good when evidence of good is unseen in your current situation? Can you believe that God is trustworthy? Will entering your unique Promised Land be worth a bit of wandering through the wilderness first? Maybe your response to God is this: *I'm not going to give you what you want if you can't give me what I need.*

What I didn't know at three years old but have discovered through maturity is this: Uncertainty provides rescue from being stuck in the familiar ways of life that keep us from moving forward into the purposes of God. Wandering into the wilderness of the unknown is God's divine reorientation, from what we know in the present to what God knows about the future. That's why God chose manna to satisfy the appetite of the Israelites for forty years instead of milk shakes and cheeseburgers. "I will rain down bread from heaven for you. The people are to go out each day and gather enough for that day. In this way I will *test them and see whether they will follow my instructions*" (Exodus 16:4, emphasis added).

MANNA FROM GOD doesn't always look like mashed potatoes, chocolate milk shakes, a job title, a brand-new condo, numbers of zeros on your paycheck, or high-thread-count sheets. In Hebrew, *manna* is defined as *What is it?* Because what sustains and causes growth doesn't often come by way of rational concrete answers, but in asking the right question, *What is it?* What is it that you desire from my life? What is it that you see within me that I am remiss to see within myself? What good might you accomplish through my uncertainty? And the current uncertainty in the world?

In our current culture of excess and overstimulation, we need manna from the hand of our Father, nothing more and nothing less. "The people of Israel went to work and started gathering, some more, some less, but when they measured out what they had gathered, those who gathered more had no extra and those who gathered less weren't short—each person had gathered as much as was needed" (Exodus 16:17–18 *The Message*). If you are asking, *What is it?*—What is this curious, unexplainable circumstance that has arrived unexpectedly in my life?—God is asking, "Do you believe that what I will provide is *enough* to sustain and shelter you?"

That childhood photo hanging above my writing desk is backlit by a window of afternoon sun illuminating my short brown curls and the white sailor collar on a blue dress. Like my brief stint with married parents, nothing about the photo is memorable or familiar—the chair I'm kneeling on, the wooden table that holds my birthday cake, the sheer glow of curtains banking the sides of the open window in the background, or the faded wooden fence beyond, outside the open door. I'm three years old, leaning over a cake, paradoxically with determination not to smile, preparing to cast a wish upon my future.

Foundations bring shape to our lives, but they don't define who we are at the core. Capturing story through photography is a spiritual practice in seeing life differently when I am prone to find comfort in familiarity. God is not slow to respond; we are slow to come around to being loved by him. Why do you think it took the Israelites forty years to reach the Promised Land when the journey could've been made in a few weeks?

The Exodus story provides a mirror and a map for navigating uncertainty for us. Think of me as your guide through the wilderness with a camera strapped over my shoulder, framing details in the following pages.

Reframe uncertainty through the lens of the certainty of God's love, and interpret current events from the perspective of promise that is never revoked. What are the images of life you are holding on to that create false narratives? What is God saying that the headlines aren't declaring? What is anxiety communicating that the Comforter is not responding to?

There is not another soul in the world who can do what you do in the unique way you do it. You are gifted with talents that God created unlike any other talent in the world. You can be compared to no one because never has your frame been thought of the same way by any two people. There is no need to compete or elbow your way into a room because your very essence speaks of God's glory. And his presence in you is a force to be reckoned with in this uncertain world. He can answer all your unknowns in a blink but he loves you by giving you a choice of response. If you are allowing uncertainty in the world to determine how useful you are to God, maybe it's time to rethink who and what is informing your value and worth.

IN THE EARLY days, while living at my grandparents' home under the care of my father, I grew into anticipating Saturday mornings as comfort. That day in the week provided the luxury of being nestled into the crook of Dad's arm under the warmth of blankets—talking, laughing, bouncing on the mattress, and playing imaginary games. But the divorce came with new rhythms, and that comfort was no longer available to me. As the days, weeks, months, and years passed, I saw less and less of Dad. His absence translated as *I'm not enough*; I assumed I wasn't worth the effort. After all, being a husband and a father wasn't what he envisioned for his life in that season. But I was wrong.

When I sent Dad the old photograph of myself bending over the frosted birthday cake, requesting the back story about the sober expression written on my face, he responded graciously in

If you are allowing *uncertainty* in the world to determine how useful you are to God, maybe it's time to *rethink* who and what is informing your *value* and *worth*.

the spirit of generosity. Risking rejection, Dad reveals the truth, reframing the uncertain season of our lives with the redemption that time and distance create. "I truly wanted to have you live with me, but things got very difficult between my parents, your mother, and myself. I could see you were being pulled in many different directions, which was causing you to be confused and hurt. I thought it best to step back and not be the father to you I wanted to be. I thought releasing you would be for the best."

My father's absence ameliorates into unselfish sacrifice with the revelation of truth captured in his vulnerability. I reply to Dad's email: "As I've pondered what you wrote, I just want you to know that I don't hold anything against you at all. I realize that you were in a terribly difficult place when I was a child, and in what I can imagine was a lot of emotional pain. I'm just sad that we missed out on having a normal father/daughter relationship. Growing up, I often translated your emotional distance as my not being wanted or loved, but knowing that the decision you made was out of love and for my good brings a lot more clarity and understanding to why things were as they were. Please don't allow the past to have a hold on you now. God has been faithful to redeem what happened for our good. I'm grateful you were willing to revisit the past knowing it was painful, difficult, and so long ago."

I learn it wasn't just becoming a father and supporting a new wife that kept my father from realizing a law degree from years of study. A priest acting as professor and later, assistant dean of the school blocked him from completing the remaining three hours he had left to finish the program. Dad never wanted to practice law in the classic sense, but what he gleaned from those years served a long, successful business career.

We are never too old, experienced, or responsible to need the certainty of our heavenly Father's love. And never too old, experienced, or responsible to misinterpret silence from God during seasons of uncertainty as unloving. Silence rings as wisdom with the luxury of time and distance. Reframing uncertainty through the lens of being deeply loved and fully known changes the way we translate adversity in beginnings and what I would come to define as a tumultuous middle.

Practice Reframing Uncertainty through the Lens of Being Known

What is the first memory you have of uncertainty in your life?

How did you respond?

With the perspective of time, what is that memory saying to you now?

How might you respond to uncertainty differently right now?

What narrative would you change about your story if you were given the freedom to rewrite an uncertain chapter with the certainty of God's love?

Name a goal you would like to reach by the time you finish the last chapter of this book.

Ask God to reveal to you how redemption looks from his perspective.

TWO

Where Is God?

When I sit beside the sea
watching a flotilla,
my mind is taken back
to the shores of a beloved
lake where mind, body, and soul
—like sails driven by wind—
slide across the surface of things.

Not by strength, nor genes,
only exhale of gust,
swathes of high summer sun
illuminate the path ahead.
I do not look back
but stand in the stern, a mariner poised,
perceiving what lies ahead.

SHOPPING AT SAKS Fifth Avenue and flying free in first class are
ghosts from the past. Mom leaves a lucrative job with TWA to
partner with her lesbian girlfriend in a nursery and florist business. We relocate to the small rural town of Sullivan, Missouri,

a few hours' drive from my grandparents' house. School clothes are purchased on layaway at Walmart and milk is now delivered to the house in glass bottles. Moving to a new place before school begins, the absence of friends leads Mom to drop me off at the public pool in the center of town, minutes after the doors open for business. Sunbathing alone, I protect my corner of concrete among throngs of strangers by maintaining the boundaries of yellow rectangular terry cloth. Beads of sweat drip from armpits and travel down my midsection as I remain stationary, concealing the lines of a maxi pad in my swimsuit bottoms. Envious of tanned legs jumping into cool, blue water, relief comes when I spot our car in the parking lot, hours later.

Once school begins and I begin making friends, I stay within the confines of the canary walls of my new teenage bedroom in the evenings. A collection of international dolls, a yellow smiley face bank, and a red velvet jewelry box decorate the shelves of white provincial furniture. Abba's "Dancing Queen" swoons from the record player, drowning out the drone of cars slithering down the gravel driveway. As sky shifts from azure to a thin black veil, I sit alone, cross-legged on a twin bed, petting Puff, a white Persian purring in my lap. Staring out the back window, my eyes land on the dilapidated empty red barn in the acreage beyond the fence. Imagination and story provide mental escape from the voices in the next room, men using expletives as adjectives when they enter the house.

On a school night, beer cans and ashtrays invade the normal yawn of the living room. And Ted Nugent's "Cat Scratch Fever" blares from the stereo, replacing the cheerful tunes of the Partridge Family. Acrid aroma of cigarettes mingles with home-grown marijuana, overwhelming the scent of Lauren cologne spritzed from the square crimson bottle as room deodorizer. Door slightly ajar creating a portal of protective witness, I glimpse familiar faces seen while walking the halls of high school, but most are strangers.

As digits on the clock scroll toward bedtime, a nightgown slips over arms stretching toward the ceiling; a ring of lace decorates my neck and ruffles graze bare ankles. Pink flannel replaces frayed bell-bottoms and my favorite kelly-green T-shirt with screen print of Elton John. Slipping naked feet underneath chilly sheets and blankets, the fur ball once warming up cold legs repositions on my chest, kneading paws into the bedspread. Sinking curly hair into feather pillow, I become a voyeur from a porthole of darkness, watching people pass through the kitchen into the bathroom. A young man stands in front of the phone hanging on the wall. Several feet of long, curly cord hangs in a loop over the chair where most telephone conversations are held, unless they are private, in which case the long length of yellow cord stretches into the bedrooms of our small country rental.

Will he choose the hallway for conversation or push the door open into the cocoon of my dark bedroom? Heart racing in anticipation, I further assess from a warm spot in bed the yellow receiver is resting on the cradle, not pushed up to his ear. It isn't the phone he wants, but the entrails of a woman's purse lying on the chair. *Wait a minute, that's my mother's purse!* I wonder if perhaps he's been tasked with buying more beer and granted permission to extract a few dollars from her wallet?

Rationale is suddenly squelched as he pillages my mother's paycheck, pushing newly cashed bills into pockets of faded jeans, jerking head from side to side, scanning the area before walking away with a sense of urgency. I am the only witness to a petty crime, and eerie quietness replaces boisterous banter in the house. Perhaps I have been dreaming this alternate universe. But Johnny Carson's familiar voice and audience laughter from the television quickly affirms that I'm indeed awake and sober-minded. The opening monologue soothes anxiety toward peaceful repose until the realization hits me: I am alone in a house at the end of an isolated stretch of dark, rural country road.

Or am I?

Blue wicker headboard knocks gently into the wall, rocking to the rhythm of fear beating from my heart as I hear something stir underneath the house, directly below my bedroom. Puff jumps off my chest, affirming what I hear is real and not imaginary.

Underneath the weathered-wood floor of my bedroom is an empty dank basement where the clothes dryer lives. The space is tidy, but cobwebs stretch from the corners of the window frames, making the emptiness feel creepy. Even in daylight, I anticipate an ugly scream or the feel of rodents crawling on the surface of my skin when I'm within the bowels of those bare concrete walls. A single light bulb hangs from the ceiling, providing quick illumination before retrieving warm clothes from the dryer, an act of bravery I perform once a week.

As I lie still in bed, listening to wind blowing in and out of my nose, something mimicking the dreaded surprise in a thriller movie is discerned. An unmistakable sucking sound on the seal of the basement door mysteriously releases, meaning someone has accessed the door from outside. We rarely use that door. Old and warped, countless layers of paint slathered over rotted wood makes the door stick and difficult to open. But determination opens the door, breaking the suffocating silence in the empty house, revving my heart up in tandem.

Those burglar boys have come back, it's my first assumption. Willing my mind toward rational thought, as a fine line exists between healthy caution and paranoia, I wonder if perhaps my mother or her girlfriend are in the basement for some unknown-to-me reason. But entering the house through the basement is an anomaly. It never happens, much less in the middle of the night.

In a frozen stance, arms crossed over my chest, I listen for the familiar cadence of voices, but hear a rustling sound rather than conversation. Footsteps on creaky wooden stairs echo from the bowels of the concrete cavern, ascending slowly upward, one slow step at a time, pausing at the top of the staircase, in front of the door that opens into the house. An entrance across the hallway that I can see clearly through the crack in my bedroom door.

The old brass doorknob jiggles as it twists from the other side. And instead of whisking out of bed to lock the bedroom door, creating a barrier between myself and the intruder, I remain still, visualizing Grandma's manicured, bony fingers rubbing the clear crystal beads of her rosary draped over her lap. Reciting the Lord's Prayer silently to myself as comfort, I imagine saying the words with her. *Our Father who art in heaven, hallowed be thy name, thy kingdom come, thy will be done, on earth as it is in heaven . . . Help me! Help me!*

MY HEART IS the mallet to the drum of a twin bed, beating fiercely to the rhythm of fear. And God's rescue comes in the form of a crude metal hook, normally hanging loose from a screw in the doorframe, but on this night, uncharacteristically latched for my salvation. Silence ensues. Footsteps retreat. Minutes later, the crescendo of gravel crunching under tires translates as relief. Headlights illuminate a shroud of inky evergreens surrounding the house, disrupting evil lurking in the shadows. Though I've been lying in bed for hours, my body is limp from exhaustion. The sound of slurred speech coming from my mother's voice provides solace, and within seconds, I drift off to sleep, far, far away from the fear of the unknown resident in my house.

Hopefully, you have never been a voyeur to a thief rummaging through your personal history. But most of us can identify with uncertainty skulking through familiar details of our lives, threatening livelihood, and creating fear about the future. It's in our afflictions—those times in life when we cannot buy, think, create, converse, or Google our way out of pain and adversity—that our formative faith is revealed as faulty, frail, or sure-footed.

The next morning, a full can of flat beer left on the kitchen counter is used as a rinse for my hair after shampooing, in an attempt to find some usefulness in the chaos of my childhood. Sage-green corduroys, bell-bottom jeans with frayed ends, and three shirts sway on wire hangers when I open the door of my small closet. Dust bunnies swirl around the wood floor and float into a lone pair of penny loafers. Staring at my clothes like they are masterpieces leaving dust marks on a cathedral wall, I exhale, tired of trying to mix and match a meager wardrobe. Mrs. Hollingshead, my English teacher, wears no makeup and rarely runs a comb through her sphagnum-moss nest of curly locks. She's attempting to make it through the entire school year without wearing the same outfit twice, creatively shifting a few simple pieces for a fresh daily look. One of her students challenged with keeping her accountable, I want to see if she can pull it off.

A wet towel twisted into a turban weighs heavy on my head as I sit on the edge of the bed my mother shares with her girlfriend, pushing my forefinger into cigarette holes in the blanket, asking for permission from Mom to wear her burgundy short-sleeved cardigan. As I open the drawer from their dresser, what I see as I glance up and look outside the window raises the hair on my forearm. A swath of sunlight refracts on the step of a metal ladder resting against the window ledge. None of us recall using a ladder recently, much less near that window.

Uncapping the gold top from the square ruby bottle of perfume on my dresser, I spritz a cloud of fragrance and watch the mist settle, veiling the musty odor of cigarette smoke. In the memory of last night's event, I pray my reputation is covered by silence from the mouths of the boys I will pass in the hallway before the tardy bill rings.

UNCERTAINTY IS NOT prejudiced; it comes to all of us equally and without bias, and we can say the same about the certainty of God's love. Most of us respond to uncertainty like the sudden discovery of an ominous ladder pushed up to the bedroom window. How did that happen? Why didn't I see that coming? What do I do now? Why is this happening to me? In the grasp of uncertainty, finding safety and achieving security becomes a high aim. All our carefully constructed coping mechanisms are exposed as frauds when the unexpected arrives. Whether you are in a dead-end job or suffering job loss; financially stressed or stressed out by national politics; suffering consequences of a natural disaster or in the disastrous aftermath of a betrayal, the fear of uncertainty is rooted in this belief: God won't meet me in the way I am desperate for him to show up. And our greatest certitude is this: God is already in the room.

"BE STILL, AND know that I am God" wrote the Sons of Korah in Psalm 46, one of eleven psalms in the Bible attributed to their creative authorship. Psalms that express gratitude, humility, and thankfulness for the attributes of an omniscient and powerful God. The phrase *Be still, and know that I am God* may be familiar to you. Perhaps a reminder of conviction by way of a meme scrolling on social media, imprinted on a mug holding your morning coffee, or from wall art hanging in your living home. I've seen *Be still* tattooed on wrists and forearms. But like a child's artwork magnetized to the refrigerator, what initially translates as revelatory and meaningful is quickly lost when art becomes commonplace.

For the Sons of Korah, *Be still, and know that I am God* wasn't written as a lofty dream or wishful aspiration, but from a real-life experience of being rescued from a waking nightmare. An event they witnessed as children through the porthole of parental folly.

Descendants of Levi, their story begins as Israelites in exile, traveling through the wilderness with their clan after leaving Egypt. The Levites were chosen by God for full-time service; ordained to take care of the tabernacle and all its implements, as well as the Ark of the Covenant. But only the descendants of Aaron, also called Aaronites, could serve as priests. Levites serve the priests in the family of Aaron in the care of the tabernacle and, later, the temple.

The three sons of Levi were Gershon, Merari, and Kohath. The Gershonites and Merarites were tasked with taking care of the specific details related to the tabernacle and tent—the equipment, poles, curtain, crossbar—while the Kohathites were entrusted with the sanctuary—ark, table, lampstand. While the Gershonites and Merarites could transport their items on carts, the Kohathites were charged with carrying the holy accoutrements on their shoulders. They bore the literal weight of transporting items from place to place as the camp moved, but they were not allowed to touch the items or death would be their fate. And as you can probably imagine, that little detail caused some issues.

The Kohathites began to grumble, "That's not fair." I mean honestly, wouldn't you?

Korah, the grandson of Kohath, began showing signs of rebellion against their fate, running with a group of Reubenite malcontents. In pride, they provoked the ire of 250 men and challenged the right of Moses and Aaron to the priesthood (Numbers 16). As a result, God's virulent anger was aroused.

The ground underneath them split apart and swallowed the Kohathites along with all their possessions. Alive. At their cries, all the Israelites around them fled, shouting, "'The earth is going to swallow us too!' And fire came out from the LORD and consumed the 250 men who were offering the incense" (Numbers 16:34–35). The event marked God's wrath due to rebellion, but it's also a story left for us with the imprint of compassion.

The Sons of Korah were the only people in their clan to be spared from being buried alive that day. I imagine them as shocked and still, waiting and watching from the chrysalis of their childhood, as they experienced the redemption of reverse mentoring—learning from the folly of their father about how *not* to live their lives as adults. The Sons of Korah grew up to become leaders of choral and orchestral music in the tabernacle during the reign of King David, penning such words as *How lovely is your dwelling place, Lord Almighty* in Psalm 84. Not only did they write the psalms, but the Sons of Korah were trusted gatekeepers, responsible for securing and protecting the tabernacle and temple. The ancestral tree of the Kohathites now begins with their DNA. Seven generations later, Samuel becomes a branch from the faithfulness the Sons of Korah propagated.

The search for certainty begins for all of us at a young age. And like the Sons of Korah, only those who truly believe they are fully known and deeply loved can sing in times of adversity. "God is our refuge and strength, an ever-present help in trouble. Therefore we will not fear, though the earth give way and the mountains fall into the heart of the sea, though its waters roar and foam and the mountains quake with their surging" (Psalm 46:1–3).

Unaware of how to name it that fateful night lying in the sanctuary of a small bedroom, I chose stillness and breath prayer as my heart surged with fear. In Hebrew, the words *be still* mean to allow yourself to become weak, to let go, surrender, and release your grip. Breath prayer is an ancient Christian practice dating back to the sixth century; it is short, repetitive prayers that become as natural as breathing and make the practice of praying without ceasing possible. The popular children's prayer—*Now I lay me down to sleep, I pray the Lord my soul to keep*—illustrates how a simple phrase recited on the inhale and exhale of breath results in peaceful repose.

Back then, it seemed as though my life was crumbling before it was beginning, yet God was creating sovereign foundations that forever changed the way I frame certainty. If you and I were to look at a map detailing the journey of our lives, rarely would we find navigation in straight, predictable lines. Intersections, interruptions, delays, unforeseen roadblocks, and sinkholes create opportunities we didn't plan or predict with the accuracy of GPS. Which is disconcerting since most of us long for surety.

Safety and security are high values for most of us. We like to know how things are going to turn out before moving ahead. Detours interrupting the paths we project for ourselves evoke the fear of uncertainty. And self-reliance is our quick fix for achieving the certainty we need to feel at peace. I once heard someone say, "I can deal with things not working out the way I envision them as long as I have a plan." And needing a backup plan to achieve inner peace really isn't faith, is it?

We sign up for blood tests predicting the sex of a baby in utero, plan the décor of a nursery based on those details. We move in with partners as a trial run before committing to marriage and write prenuptial agreements in case things don't work out. We want to know a place is safe before we visit, and a home is secure before our children spend the night. We like the assurance of how money will be used by a homeless stranger before placing coins in her open palms.

Being safe isn't wrong and seeking security isn't sinful, but according to God, achieving comfort isn't a priority to him. He doesn't promise safety and security; he promises that he will be with you (Exodus 3:12–15). Reframing safety through the lens of being fully known and deeply loved can be captured in the mnemonic

S-urrender (to the)
A-lmighty
F-or
E-ternal perspective

As Moses was tasked with leading the Israelites out of captivity, God's presence was sure, yet he still doubted himself in making their freedom a reality. The holiness of God was made manifest in the horrific moment Moses witnessed his cousins, the Sons of Korah, become orphans. For me, holy love manifested in an empty house at the end of a dirt road, my body quaking in fear, uncertain about the future.

You are not forgotten. God is with you in exile, isolation, aloneness, and loneliness. He is present as you wade through the unknowns that make up your wilderness journey.

Life for me began uncertain, insecure, and unstable. But if you were to assess my life now through the portal of Instagram, that might be a surprising revelation. Photos of gingerbread houses, colorful doors, verdant parks, and decadent flower carts might lead you to assume that making my home as a committed migrant in England came by way of a straight, satisfying line labeled *idyllic*. Anguishing twists and gut-wrenching turns are unseen beyond the borders of those neat, tidy squares in my gallery. But the more I look back and survey the past, it is the hidden intimacies with God that stand out as my most memorable captures. Looking at life through the lens of being fully known and deeply loved brings the beauty of redemption into focus. That's why my husband, H, and I call ourselves committed migrants rather than American expats: Fully committed to the people and places where God sends us, our posture is open and receptive rather than closed-fisted.

As I capture the history of the Sons of Korah, honing in on details foundational to their story within the big sweeping landscape of the Exodus, that shallow depth of field provides greater depth of insight and meaning. At first glance, it seems random that the Sons of Korah were being led by Moses through the wilderness as exiles, but they share more in common than ancestral heritage. Moses and the Sons of Korah share uncertain beginnings, childhood adversity, growing up in the presence of royalty, and being used as God's messengers. Through the lens of their unique stories, I can see how uncertainty has provided opportunity for encountering God's love and friendship as certain—close and intimate—when at times, it seemed as though he was distant, uncaring, and ambivalent.

> You are not *forgotten*. God is with you in exile, isolation, aloneness, and *loneliness*.

As we wrestle with layers of political, economic, and social uncertainties, continual unrest might be translated as God retreating from the chaos. But in exploring the Exodus story, it is revelatory to remember that Moses entered the world during a tumultuous time in history, the circumstances surrounding his birth translated as hopeless by many. According to Pharaoh, Moses' fate was to be thrown into the Nile River before taking his first steps.

"The king of Egypt said to the Hebrew midwives, whose names were Shiphrah and Puah, 'When you help the Hebrew women in childbirth and observe them on the delivery stool, if you see that the baby is a boy, kill him; but if it is a girl, let her live'" (Exodus 1:15–16). But Shiphrah and Puah were fiercely bravehearted and feared God more than the wrath of Pharaoh, committing the first documented act of civil disobedience. They refused to carry out his wishes. And God responded to their trust and faithfulness with abundance. "God was kind to the midwives and the people increased and became even more numerous. And because the midwives feared God, he gave them families of their own" (Exodus 1:20–21).

Kohath was the ancestor of Amram. The name of Amram's wife was Jochebed, a descendant of Levi, born as an exile to Levi in Egypt and Moses' mother (Numbers 26:58–59). But unlike Kohath, Jochebed didn't allow circumstances to dictate her actions. She possessed spiritual acumen that translated uncertainty differently. Floating her baby inside a basket bed rather than drowning him, she effectively ushered Moses into the arms of royalty. The Hebrew word for the basket used to save Moses' life is the same word used for the ark that preserved Noah, the only blameless man, and his family. God was not only rescuing one baby boy, or even one nation, but redeeming the whole of creation through Moses and Israel. And the release of abundance was echoed by God when Jochebed retrieved Moses and against all odds nursed him into childhood.

Your uncertainty is God's opportunity to release the abundance planned for your life. What if we responded like Jochebed and the midwives when we read headlines, tweets, and social media rants? What Miriam didn't say about Moses being her brother; what Jochebed didn't say about the baby she was nursing being her own son; what the midwives chose not to say about baby boys being born—translates as wisdom ushering in the favor of God. Sometimes *not* speaking takes more faith than spilling what you know. What if we translated current events through the lens of being loved by the Almighty who holds time in his hands? What if you and I were part of the few who interpret tumult and chaos as opportunity for God to reveal himself? What abundance might we be missing by going with the flow and basing future outcomes on today's popular mind-sets?

The writer of Hebrews tells us that it is faith in the unseen that changes the world. "By faith Moses' parents hid him for three months after he was born, because they saw he was no ordinary child, and they were not afraid of the king's edict" (Hebrews 11:23). Faith in the unseen looks radical to a world that uses what is seen as predictors for future outcomes. And lack of fear reveals where the certainty of your trust is placed. But without godly discernment, we cannot discern the extraordinary. Without identifying God's extraordinary presence amid upheaval, faith and fear become muddled. Following in the footsteps of his parents, Moses refused the safety and security associated with being the son of Pharaoh's daughter, and instead chose a lesser, hidden life, preferring disgrace for the sake of Christ over wealth and privilege. "He persevered because he saw him who is invisible" (Hebrews 11:27).

Faith is complete trust or confidence in someone or something. Complete, meaning *to have all the necessary or appropriate parts.* What part of God are you unsure about? Faith is impossible without being acquainted with the necessary parts of God's nature and character that allow you to trust him. The entirety of

Your uncertainty
is God's *opportunity*
to release the
abundance planned
for your life.

who he is was finished when his Son was crucified on the cross of Calvary for you.

Before Moses was tasked as God's messenger, leading the Israelites out of captivity to wander through the desert, he encountered God in a field, with the sound of sheep bleating in the distance. A flame rather than a flower garnered his attention, and the aperture of his understanding was opened in a voice calling, "Moses! Moses!" You could say that both Moses and the Sons of Korah experienced God's extraordinary presence and discerned a life that was different from the norm.

How differently might our lives look today had Moses walked away from the burning bush instead of choosing to follow God through the wilderness? Thankfully, Moses wasn't relying on self-assurance; the assurance of God's presence guided Moses through the uncertainties of the journey. How differently might Moses' story read had his mother chosen self-reliance over a reliance on God? How differently might verses in the Psalms read had the Sons of Korah chosen self-focus over an unlikely focus on God's faithfulness? How differently might your story read by choosing to reframe uncertainty with the certainty of God's presence with you?

God entrusted oversight of the Israelites to Moses, not because he needed a challenge or a break from routine, but because God saw a greater depth of field within Moses than Moses was seeing within himself. If you were to apply depth of field as a metaphor for your story, every situation you encounter provides an opportunity on where to focus. Will you focus on what you have right in front of you—God's presence—or will you trust in your humanity to navigate the unknowns of your wilderness journey? Where you choose to focus determines how you arrive. Depth of field is a worldview we choose: either an interpretation through the way the world frames the headlines, or through the lens of God's character and nature as discovered in Scripture. As Christians, our field of view should expand beyond spatial orientation. Spiritual eyes that capture

God's angle on current culture from an eternal perspective. The spiritual practice of choosing to focus on the attributes of God will help calm anxiety and identify Truth among voices competing for influence.

The aperture of God's love was open wide for the Sons of Korah and for me, while growing into adulthood, schooled by the foolishness and missteps of others. Because God sees a future we are incapable of envisioning as children. If depth of field is determined by where you focus, is God far away or close in your circumstances? Is uncertainty creating a barrier or a bridge to intimacy with Him?

Be still, and know that I am God; I will be exalted among the nations, I will be exalted in the earth. It's a certainty I cling to inside the dark chrysalis of uncertain beginnings, and later, when I spread my wings, take flight, and emerge into British culture, taking up residence in London, England.

Practice BREATH PRAYER
FOR THE WILDERNESS OF FEAR

Read the story of the Sons of Korah in Numbers 16. If you could sum up the theme of their story, what would that be?

What details in the story of the Sons of Korah are new revelation for you?

How does their story inform your own?

Where is God in your story? Near or distant?

Read Psalm 46 from the perspective of the author's history. How does the psalm translate when you know the back story?

Practice using Psalm 46:10 as a breath prayer this week—on a commute, during a lunch break, at daybreak or dusk—to summon the presence of God into your circumstances. On the inhale: *Be still.* On the exhale: *I know that you are God.*

Read Psalm 18 and Psalm 145. What do you know to be true from Scripture about the nature and character of God?

THREE

Shhh! Be Still

Rest and discern
Church bells ringing
Birds singing
Radiators creaking, strange
Voices whispering
Heels clicking on concrete, rushed.

WE ARRIVE IN London blurry-eyed from a lack of sleep, bone-tired after moving out of our spacious, open-floor-plan house in the United States. Standing in Arrivals at Heathrow, shivering in the cold, yesterday's morning view of the sun-drenched Atlantic on the South Carolina coast already feels like a long-ago, faded memory. Hovering between H and Harrison, six suitcases holding essentials create a low wall around us. Scanning a row of cars waiting to pick up passengers, I search for a familiar face, but no one is making eye contact. The liminal space between the comfort we left behind in the U.S. and the uncomfortable unknowns in the UK feels hollow as we stand still in trust, waiting for transport.

Landing in London is one of the riskiest decisions H and I have made since marrying three decades ago. We left a beloved job, 75 percent of our yearly income, three thousand square feet, the ability to drive a car anytime we want, two-thirds of our personal belongings, and our daughter in her first year of college. We left all that and a lot more to fulfill a ministry call to London. Basically, we willfully left certainty to enter the most stressful, uncertain season of our lives. We didn't have a compass for the what, where, when, and how in our journey to London. God was more interested in keeping us in the mystery.

Tim jumps out of a red car, smiling broadly, extending arms open in welcome. At last! We have not been forgotten. He is the vicar of St. Barnabas Kensington Church and shares in the responsibility of bringing us across the pond. He's been prayerful, faithful, and patient in preparing the church for our arrival through the narrow passage of a bureaucratic process. "Wait a little longer" was the mantra we heard repeatedly for nine months, until my faith nearly mutated into resignation. I feared hope would be stillborn.

H buckles into the passenger's seat next to Tim, and Harrison and I climb into the backseat, exchanging wide-eyed glances that communicate the same thing: *We made it! It's real. We are really going to live in London; it's not just a dream imagined, or wishful thinking.* But before we pull away from the curb, Tim sheepishly admits something surprising. Navigation, it turns out, isn't his strength; it's a role often acquiesced to his wife. But that morning Jan stayed behind at home, making allowances for space in the car. Fumbling with a paper map, Tim seems lost without a copilot.

"I know how to get us there," H says, pointing while giving verbal instructions with confidence, as if he's been a Londoner all his livelong life. As Tim navigates the busy streets of his hometown by the sound of H's voice, I sense our first exchange upon British soil is a foreshadowing of what is to come for us.

Winging our way from the airport to the busy motorways, the trees look as though they've been sprinkled with confetti.

We left palm trees swaying in the warm breeze and arrived at tiny white and pink flowers decorating branches and blanketing the ground around trunks. The metaphors are all around us, declaring, "Welcome to a new season!"

Times of uncertainty are like dormancy during winter. We may not see tangible evidence of where we are going, what God is doing, or how we are growing, but wintering is essential preparation for life to flourish. Uncertainty, like winter, clears the landscape of familiarity so we can see ourselves clearly as Christ's masterpiece, bringing value and beauty into the world. Renewal is the outcome of trust in God's hidden work within us. And my heart is renewed by stilling images from the Exodus story.

Before Moses was tasked with leading the Israelites out of Egypt, his leadership experience on a résumé could have read: tended borrowed sheep on land owned by his wife's father; isolated in a strange place for forty years. And the Israelites weren't equipped with prior experience or familiar maps on making the transition from enslavement to freedom either. Everything about the Exodus journey was new, unfamiliar, and rife with uncertainty. And the route God chose from Egypt to the Promised Land must have led the Israelites to scratch their heads in conundrum rather than rejoice in celebration. Because, "When Pharaoh let the people go, God did not lead them on the road through the Philistine country, though that was shorter. For God said, 'If they face war, they might change their minds and return to Egypt.' So God led the people around by the desert road to the Red Sea" (Exodus 13:17–18).

The promises of God to us are rarely realized by traveling in familiar, straight lines without inclines, roadblocks, or interruptions. Not one of us can claim the epitaph *All I envisioned for my life came to pass in exactly the way I planned it.* God often chooses the long way around over the easy, concrete shortcuts because wandering leads to Red Sea moments, those times when life becomes completely out of your control and under the control of God's powerful presence. While that out-of-control feeling isn't a goal for any of us, is there a better place to be than under the control of God's providence? But I'm human, like the Israelites, and the more I looked at the circumstances greeting us in London, the more I began to doubt God's goodness.

> God often chooses the *long way* around over the easy, concrete shortcuts because *wandering* leads to Red Sea moments.

We live from suitcases lying on the worn carpet of a temporary house boasting high ceilings, low furniture, big windows, and small sinks. We trade decorator furniture for a mismatched musty sofa and broken file drawer used as an end table. Flip-flops and carefree walks on the beach mutate into wearing boots, carrying umbrellas, and becoming vigilant about time while using Google maps for train and bus schedules. An oyster is no longer associated with outdoor roasts in a seaside village, but a card that allows access to public transportation among the masses. Instead of filling up a gas tank, we fill our eyes with British culture from the window seat on the second story of a red double-decker bus. Basically, I follow H's head and shoulders wherever we go, thanking God he is six foot four, standing out as a beacon when I fear being lost.

I make grocery lists from memorized recipes because all the grease-stained, reliable cookbooks are in a box stacked inside a crate that is sailing on a ship somewhere in the Atlantic. How Pollyanna of me to think temporary housing means I can temporarily avoid cooking and cleaning dishes. Planning and preparing meals are second nature since marrying H, but my first trip to the grocery store in London makes me feel like a newlywed again. Nothing feels familiar. Well, to be clear, sugar, potatoes, and bread *look* familiar, but caster, Maris Piper, and whole meal require translation. A seemingly simple shopping trip to fill an empty pantry and refrigerator mutates into a three-hour tutorial by Jan on *How to Shop for Groceries in England*. And culture shock doesn't end when we unload a full boot of groceries from the car into the house.

Chili is what's for dinner because it's easy and familiar like pizza on Friday or grilling on a warm weekend. Temperatures plummet and I can almost smell the aroma of chili seasoning mingling with tomato sauce wafting through the house, awakening us with familiarity. Creating a cozy atmosphere inside a drafty house is the goal, but the easy recipe I choose proves more difficult than first assumed.

The little brown seasoning box with the red label isn't available in the spice aisle, so I Google *chili seasoning* and decide to make my own concoction. But I quickly discover that we have no measuring spoons, a little detail missed in the essential items packed in my suitcase. H retrieves a digital scale someone left in the kitchen cabinet and I survey a conversion chart. But we learn the battery is dead. Onion powder is missing from the spices collected on that life-altering grocery trip. H zips up his coat and dashes to the corner market but returns empty-handed after scouring shelves of several stores in the neighborhood. We can make chili without onion powder. What can it hurt?

Kidney beans are lined up on the counter, but they are useless for the recipe when, after sifting through drawers in the kitchen, I discover we have no can opener (*tin opener* in British). What I chose as a familiar family recipe to make for dinner mutates into a hard, complicated task.

When we moved to London, I never imagined that the simple things that kept me grounded while waiting through a lengthy, bureaucratic process would be a source of anxiety after landing. Planning meals, grocery shopping, simple conversation, not to mention phone numbers with eleven digits sans dashes: Hello! How am I supposed to memorize that? But navigating the mundane things of life in a new culture are no match for learning how to parent our daughter, Murielle, across an ocean. Because the certainty of our faith is tested by disruption.

Seated in brown plastic chairs around the dinner table, we scoop spoonsful of steaming chili into bowls and place them on tiny cork placemats. The empty fourth chair pushed under the table across from me makes Murielle's absence a noticeable vacuum. I miss her presence and the familiar flavor of interaction between us. Luckily, the magic of using apps isn't lost on us, keeping communication open and current in our new context.

Coming home to reconnect with family on a school break is no longer an option for our firstborn. Murielle's former bedroom, layered with stuffed animals, school awards, and childhood mementos, lives in boxes stacked in a storage unit. On spring break, she borrows a bed at a friend's house and Voxes with an admission. She's been driving to our empty house daily, sitting cross-legged on the carpet in silence, and waiting for the reality of our departure to hit. But the tears refuse to fall.

While in the middle of a meeting with church planters in East London, H leans over and tells me that he's received an official email from our Realtor—our house in Pawleys Island, South Carolina, is no longer in our possession. It's an ending we've been praying for, for months. The sale is official! We send a message to Murielle, alerting her to the new reality. The key to the front door is now a keepsake, no longer useful for finding comfort in our absence.

A few days later, I am awakened in the early morning hours, lying next to H in the stillness of a strange house, aware that my body is blazing with fever. Praying for my children when I am unable to fall back to sleep, I hear H's phone vibrate from the nightstand on his side of the bed. I assume, because of the time difference, it's a random notification from social media. I choose not to awaken him. When sunlight finally floods through the bedroom window, every muscle aches, telling me that my body is sick with influenza. H looks at his phone and discovers the vibration I heard was a Vox sent by Murielle. As he listens, phone up to his ear, I can hear Murielle's frantic voice from the recording.

We learn that on the drive back to college, she is alone on the side of a back road with a blown tire in the void of inky darkness. She's been stranded for three hours. Normally, H would have jumped in the car, showed up with tools and a spare tire. But we are lying in bed, an ocean away from where she is weeping on the side of the road. And I'm not sure I've ever experienced this much regret or felt this helpless as a parent.

Why? It's the first question I ask of God. *Why are you allowing this to happen? Why is our yes to you resulting in distress for our daughter? What certainty can I claim when the unknowns are overwhelming? How can I find peace without knowing how this story is going to play out?*

Resurrection is free and it costs you something. New beginnings are God's specialty; yours for the price of an uncomfortable waiting period and birthed with God's magnificent question, "Do you trust me?" Will you trust God's plan is good when the plan is less economical, beautiful, or organized than what you envisioned? Will you trust God when a new job comes with a pay cut? A demotion? Leaving home, country, and family? Downsizing instead of expanding? Lack that leaves you feeling helpless to help others?

New *beginnings* are God's specialty; yours for the price of an *uncomfortable* waiting period and *birthed* with God's magnificent question, "Do you trust me?"

When released from life as you know it into an uncomfortable transition period, God will not lead you by way of a shortcut. Bypass the wilderness and your trust becomes dependent on this wrong assumption: Safety and security equals God's favor and my happiness. Perhaps secure as defined by God's heart can be summed up in this mnemonic:

S-et apart
E-stablished as an heir
C-herished
U-nderstood
R-escued
E-mbraced by the Lord of lords

Give in to the wars waging without and miss the abundance of peace available within. Being safe and secure as defined by the world isn't God's highest aim. The Westminster Catechism states that *man's chief end is to glorify God and enjoy him forever.* Your uncertainty is an opportunity to practice giving God glory and enjoy him in the wilderness. In my case, the desert of sickness, helpless to help my firstborn.

H AND HARRISON practice walking over miles of cracks on pavement, becoming acquainted with London, while I memorize cracks in the ceiling of my new bedroom, forced into rest by sickness. The worn carpet beneath the mattress is a canvas of crumpled tissues and boxes of Lemsip, Beechams, and Paracetemol. Even the names of over-the-counter medications are foreign to me. While the Israelites wandered through the desert, hemmed in by unwanted circumstances, they cried out, "Was it because there were no graves in Egypt that you brought us to the desert to die? What have you done to us by bringing us out of Egypt? Didn't we say to you in Egypt, 'Leave us alone; let us serve the Egyptians'? It would have been better for us to serve the Egyptians than to die in the desert!" (Exodus 14:11–12).

Relating to the Israelites, it became tempting to look at my untimely sickness and Murielle's vulnerable situation during our first days of separation and conclude God's abandonment. I began to believe my own bad press, assuming he left us to fend for ourselves after we agreed to follow him to London. The search for certainty becomes my addiction. No matter how much we know or how long we live, we are not immune to learning the same lesson all over again. I admit that I echo the whining Israelites often, especially when plans don't fall as easily into place as I envision them.

Why did you bring us to London now if you knew the flu would keep me bedridden? Why would you solve my loneliness with a move across the ocean, where I am alone, separated from my family? Why make us exiles from the U.S., only to alienate us from our daughter? Perhaps we heard you wrong. Maybe it would be better for us to go back to what is familiar?

Maybe you are in the middle of a Red Sea moment too? All you can see in front of you is what you don't have. You can't identify God's presence while weighed down by stress. Perhaps abundance seems like something you only read about in storybooks? Are you tempted to go back to Egypt and rely on the familiar as comfort, even though you know that kind of certainty isn't God's best for you?

Allow the presence of God to be the bridge through your uncertainty. The axis of uncertainty is disorientation, and let's face it, who wants to be spinning in all directions while in transition? Research tells us it is more settling for us to prepare for a bad outcome than not having a clue about where we will end up. But what if the axis of uncertainty is a reorientation back to God's love—stable, steadfast, and secure—preparing you to receive his promises? Could you wander with him if fulfilling purpose and claiming abundance is the point of the journey through uncertainty?

In the ninth century, three Irishmen declared, "Yes!" They boarded coracles—small, lightweight, roundish boats consisting of a simple basket frame, seat, waterproof cover—and courageously drifted over the sea from Ireland for seven days without oars. Can you imagine?!

Coming ashore in Cornwall, they were brought to the court of King Alfred. When the king interrogated the three Irish teachers about their obscure journey, they replied that they "stole away because we wanted for the love of God to be on pilgrimage, we cared not where."[1]

Peregrinatio is a little-known Celtic word used by St. Augustine of Hippo. He urged Christians in the fourth and fifth centuries to practice peregrinatio as a central way of life and faith. The word means *leaving one's homeland and wandering for the love of God.* An insatiable love for Christ did indeed drive hundreds of Celts to go forth in quest, embarking on a pilgrimage that was as much an inner journey as an outward adventure exploring new frontiers.[2]

Is it possible for those of us living today to reclaim the heart of peregrinatio? A daily quest of courage undertaken not only to exotic places, but sifting through uncertainties; choosing to be okay with inconstancy rather than stability. Ready to go wherever the Spirit is moving, even if it takes us to the wilderness?

BEFORE ARRIVING ON British soil, I stood face-to-face with my son, in the middle of a metaphorical swinging rope bridge that was a bureaucratic process with the Church of England, and discerned that Harrison innately possesses the heart of a peregrini. Waiting for leaders to dot I's and cross T's on paperwork providing passage to London, he remains steadfast in faith, assured, and positive, providing balance to our emotional ups and downs every time another delay is issued.

Initially in sensing a call to London, we assume our departure will coincide with the beginning of the British school calendar commencing in September. Harrison was at peace with a one-month gap from classes beginning at Waccamaw High School in Pawleys Island, where he had been attending high school. Instead, while his classmates carry backpacks of fresh spiral notebooks into hallways and donning the latest shoe trends, Harrison is at home with us, awaiting an imminent departure. He sleeps in, plays video games on the flat screen, researches schools in London, and puts off obtaining a learner's permit to drive a car since Brits navigate on the other side of the road.

With every response from Tim of "wait a little longer," H and I vacillate between enrolling Harrison late at Waccamaw or embarking upon homeschooling, wondering if we are ruining his life or wandering into a life-giving adventure. Everything in us as parents wants to DO something to fix the situation for Harrison, but we keep hearing, "Trust me," as the answer. With every day that passes, I assess that waiting in trust is more uncomfortable than acting in fear.

By the time we are standing on the curb at Heathrow Airport, Harrison has missed eight months of his sophomore year. And arriving late in the British school system means most of the best places in London are filled with very long waiting lists of students. We learn from empathetic influencers at church who want to help us sort the details out quickly, that there are more schools for girls than boys, which means finding a spot in a school for Harrison will require no small miracle. We are fulfilling a dream—living in London—and that translates as miraculous. Surely God didn't relocate us across an ocean to ruin our son's life?

After a week of nursing my sick body back to health, H is pulling a sweater over his head, pushing keys into pockets, and lacing up shoes from the edge of the bed where I am lying, surrounded by crumpled tissues. "You need to find Harrison a school today," he tells me, matter of fact, like making note that it's rubbish collection day and I need to put the bags out. A quick statement that seems uncharacteristically flippant because he's the decision-maker, the go-to leader of our home; the one who maps our vacations and navigates new territory. He is a pioneer, but for me, change requires determination when I am weak and slow to come to confidence.

Assigned with making a decision that will affect my son's future and interpretation of our move to London, I come to realize, is God's subversive plan to release me from the fear of uncertainty. Sickness has mutated into avoidance. I can listen to fear, stay safe in the familiarity of my new bedroom and delay immersion, or risk wandering into the unknown with him. In the practice of stilling the frames of the journey that led us to London, I am reminded that safety and security aren't God's highest aim for his children. Safety and security are not the point of bringing us to London. Surety is not the point of bringing you and me into the world. The more I experience God's character and nature, being sure takes on new definition.

S-ensing the
U-nusual
R-andom and
E-xtraordinary presence of God

Pushing myself up from the bed to standing, I hobble to an empty crooked chair in the corner of the bedroom, sit down, and ask God for favor and discernment. And dial Chelsea Academy, the name of a Church of England school scribbled on a piece of scrap paper by a member of St. Barnabas during a lunch conversation, an event organized to welcome us to the church family. After introducing myself to the English voice on the other end of the phone, I discern that my American accent is obvious and welcome to the British school administrator. She has curiously answered the phone for the receptionist and tells me that just moments before I called, a student in Harrison's year came into her office announcing he won't be returning after Easter. "We have a list of over two hundred names waiting for a place, though," she reveals. "But because your husband is a vicar with the Church of England, Harrison will be number one in the queue. Can you come to the school and complete some paperwork?"

THE CERTAINTY OF God's love is a humbling realization; a revelation on how quickly we can be led by the fear of uncertainty to assume the worst will be our life sentence. Wandering in the desert for forty years broke the Israelites' dependence on the predictable life patterns they'd grown accustomed to while enslaved in Egypt. But wandering through the wilderness wasn't aimless, careless, casual, or irresponsible; no, quite the opposite. God was leading the Israelites into the certainty of freedom and abundance. But focusing on the uncertainty in circumstances along the way kept them from believing in the certainty of God's goodness. Defining life by what you lack turns your heart and head backward toward nostalgia. And nostalgia keeps you stuck in the past rather than living life in the present. When you are committed to the place and people where you live, the sacrament of presence ushers in the holiness of God, expanding the kingdom. Referring to ourselves as expats means the heart and mind are separated between two places, not fully present or engaged here or there. In what place is God calling you to be faithful? Whom are the people God is waiting for you to engage with in your neighborhood?

Wandering is purposeful when planned by God. But how do we discern his plans from our own? We wander into new careers, marriage with a person we love, parenting kids, buying a home for the first time, and planning exotic trips, but if we are not wandering into the soul and seeking God first, then wandering into new things becomes an exploration into more lostness. How do we find our way home without a providential passport?

Maybe you are stuck in a cycle of chronic restlessness? A bevy of unknowns keep you in the same unfulfilling places and relationships. Perhaps striving for certainty makes you less certain and more frustrated? Stuck in nostalgia, longing for what was or could have been, do you have doubts about the future? Perhaps you secretly wonder if God is a generous Father to everyone but you?

Seasons of uncertainty can translate as exile from what you long for, separated from love because you don't measure up somehow. But the story of the Exodus reveals the opposite. God chooses wandering through the mystery of the wilderness, not because you have missed the mark, but because he longs for you to experience the certainty of his love. "As you do not know the path of the wind, or how the body is formed in a mother's womb, so you cannot understand the work of God, the Maker of all things" (Ecclesiastes 11:5).

Knowing that you are known by God in the unknowns of life reorients focus from self, back to the father-heart of God. Your life is only hopeless when you consider yourself helpless. "The Lord your God is God, the faithful God who keeps covenant and steadfast love with those who love him and keep his commandments, to a thousand generations" (Deuteronomy 7:9 ESV).

Our normal physiological response to uncertainty is fight or flight. But God tells us the prescription for the fear of uncertainty isn't doing more or changing circumstances. He says, "Do not be afraid. Stand firm and you will see the deliverance the Lord will bring you today. . . . The Lord will fight for you; *you need only to be still*" (Exodus 14:13–14, emphasis added).

> Your life is only *hopeless* when you consider yourself *helpless*.

When we're overwhelmed, afraid, and feeling vulnerable, the Lord tells us to stand firm in belief and be still in trust. And then he tells us to wander. "Why are you crying out to me? Tell the [people] to get moving" (Exodus 14:15).

Be still and move on? I don't know about you, but that feels like an impossibility. How does a mother stay still and move on when her daughter is an ocean away with a flat tire, alone in the middle of nowhere? How does a parent stay still when her son's future hangs in the balance of her life transition?

Maybe you are navigating an impossible scenario of your own too. How can a father be still and move on after receiving a notice of job elimination? How can a woman be still and move on after being told she won't have children? Is it possible to be still and move on when your bills are more than your income? Or your child is on a destructive path?

In photography, a still image communicates meaning. Sometimes referred to as freeze frame, these images provide details that lead to greater insight. Use of space, body language, facial expression, and feelings become more evident, adding dimension to the subject matter. God uses stillness as a process providing clarity about who you are and who he is to you. The familiar statement "A picture paints a thousand words" is truth and wisdom.

Think of stilling a frame of your life like capturing a snapshot from God's storyboard with your name as the title in big, bold letters. How might stilling this scene you're currently living provide definition for the big picture? Like a photographer looking through a viewfinder, allow God to reframe what you are currently experiencing through the lens of Truth and being known by him. What is the truth in your circumstance? What is God saying to you in the silence of preferred outcomes? What are you missing in the hurry for closure? How is God using uncertainty to shape your values about life, faith, family, relationships, work, and rest?

Still the moving pieces of your situation and capture fear and hesitancy differently. Think of contrasts in your story like the composition of a photograph, giving definition rather than detracting from the beauty. "Contrasts—warm to cold, high to low, shadow to brightness, slick to rough; without each we lose the meaning of the other in this mortal life. Without struggle and storm, the smooth, sunlit days would dream along, serene and unremarkable, taken for granted. If on a scale of one to ten everything is a ten, then a ten has no meaning, except in heaven. It carries significance only if we contrast it with a one or a two. Without the dark, hopeless stretches in our emotional and spiritual seasons, we might get bored with blessing. Grace might seem stale," writes Luci Shaw.[3] In stillness, we find illumination, clarity, and epiphany, the revealing of light as revelation. Peace and new perspective are often the result. Through the practice of identifying still frames in your story, God's character and nature become moonlight for the mystery.

As I release the need for certainty as a sign for moving forward, I wander into the unknown of a busy urban environment and get lost on streets without landmarks of familiarity. But the more I wander in faith, confidence and belief follow. Soon, I'm navigating public transportation like a boss.

In the practice of stillness, I discern truth in the mystery. God is working all things together for the good of our family, not because all the circumstances of a cross-cultural move are falling neatly into place, but because we are fully known and deeply loved by the Creator of our future. Where can we wander that God is not with us? Where can we wander that the wonder of God's love is not in our midst?

Be still in trust and steadfast in belief; only then will you be ready to wander into a spacious place—a strange place you could've never predicted as becoming home for you.

Practice STILLNESS
FOR THE WILDERNESS OF ANXIETY

Read Exodus chapters 13 and 14.

What are the frames of Moses' story that provide clarity, insight, and revelation for you?

Practice stilling a frame in your current uncertainties. Reframe the unknowns with being fully known and deeply loved by God. How does that nuance in your thinking change perspective about your situation?

What expectations are you holding that God is asking you to release?

How might your need for certainty be an idol replacing God in your situation?

Write down the visceral responses you are experiencing due to uncertainty. Still your mind by releasing each one of them back to him. In which of the scenarios causing anxiety is God not present with you?

Read Psalm 23. Rehearse the truth of God's character back to him through adoration. How do his attributes inform your circumstances?

If God is working all things together for your good, how might your untimely uncertainty be God's good timing for you?

FOUR

Breaking Habits

Not only does love show
me the way home
love bridges the way
from being alone
to companionable flesh and bone

Life is a sojourn,
not a conversation with self alone.

SKY IS DETERMINED to stay sullen and misty for consecutive days in the Cotswolds, but a crack of morning sunlight pushes the drab curtain back, revealing pastoral beauty through the picture window. Picking up my camera from the kitchen table, I skip down stone steps, stop, and snap frames of dahlias and anemones before embarking on an amble among sheep.

Past hedgerows of brambles hiding a breakfast of blackberries for sparrows, far away from the familiarity of the United States, I find myself alone on a dirt path overlooking an upturned potato field in the charming English countryside. An autumnal chill in the air and brisk breeze cause an instinctual wrapping of both arms around my waist, holding in warmth. Sheep bleat in the distance and a flock of blackbirds fly en masse from a utility wire, alighting on a patch of fallow earth. Bending over, I pull the camera up to my face, rest my eye on the viewfinder, and focus tightly on a flat oval of white Queen Anne's lace, magnifying a million tiny lace caps. And my heart wilts. The familiar sensitivity of missing my grandparents releases water into the wells of eyelids, making the intricate petals a blur of white and forest.

In PHOENIX, WHERE I met H three decades ago, my wedding bouquet boasted sprigs of Queen Anne's lace purchased for a hefty price. But in Missouri, Queen Anne's lace grows wild and profuse, rooted in the ditches flanking Interstate 44, between St. Louis and the Lake of the Ozarks. A car journey I repeat every summer as a child with my grandparents.

In St. Louis, the bedroom where Grandpa hangs collared shirts and displays a provenance of aftershaves, gifts from me since the dawn of Old Spice, is referred to as *Shelly's room* when I sleep over on weekends. The spines of Grimm's fairy tales line a small shelf of a bureau, and a collection of board games are neatly stacked behind sliding doors. But in the top drawer of the dresser, a pair of party glasses with slits for eyes are kept hidden, worn by Grandpa on the occasions of my being locked out of the house, on purpose. His highest aim was to make me laugh, and opening the front door in those crazy glasses was a sure bet to instigate giggles. Magnified eyes painted on the glasses startled me anew every time he welcomed me with ebullience at the door. And then there were the mornings of playful chases, down the hallway and through the living room to the safety of Grandma's legs, as Grandpa threatened to kiss my tiny pink cheeks with a full beard of shaving cream. Shrieks of laughter filled up the halcyon season of their lives in a quiet house.

After my parents' divorce, I lived as a character caught between two stories. During the week, after-school hours were spent in the homes of babysitters' families as I awaited Mom's pickup after work, anxious about what she might bring home from the grocery store in a brown paper bag, fearing her mercurial disposition. On the weekend, I was doted on by two people who were tirelessly faithful to each other. Nestled underneath freshly washed cotton sheets, I crawled into bed after the Saturday Primetime lineup, ending with the hilarious comedic skits by Carol Burnett and Tim Conway. I often wondered which it was, the television show or my incessant giggles, that instigated laughter between them. At bedtime, head lying on a fluffy pillow, Grandma bent over my face and brushed each of my eyebrows with her forefinger, imploring me to *never pluck them out.* Kissing my forehead, she always reminded me to say prayers before drifting off to sleep. During the summer, weekends stretched into weeklong vacations in a one-room cabin for the three of us at the Lake of the Ozarks. Fishing, swimming, eating out, and seeing the sights, it was as if I was their only priority in the checkbook and calendar. As I entered the teen years, our vacations were upgraded to the Ponderosa resort with adjoining hotel rooms, complete with indoor/outdoor pool and permission to bring a friend along. For some, Queen Anne's lace is passed over as a pesky weed. But for me, it is a beautiful, specifically placed sign of love and belonging. Of God waving from the ditches when I am seeking assurances, even assurances I am unaware that I need.

Growing up, we learn to look for signs of love and belonging through the tangible and concrete. Knowing smiles, kisses and hugs, special meals cooked, and favorite outings planned just because. As adults, those signs are often passed over like frames documenting family portraits hanging in the stairwell. They become familiar and less significant as daily responsibilities swell. But no matter what age, we are the children of God and we can identify signs of his love and belonging through the practice of his presence. The more we engage, the more likely we are to discern his whereabouts. As it is with each significant relationship cultivated in life, the signs of God's love will appear as unique to you and me. The key to finding God in the disruptions of life is intimacy and attentiveness.

We have miraculously, providentially transitioned to living as residents in England, the place where our hearts swoon with cultural affinity and kindred value systems. And yet, moving forward into the new feels like a few steps backward. From H standing on platforms among crowds of familiar faces to sitting in the back row, unknown to British influencers. From being a spiritual architect for a church planting movement in North America to culling paperwork, performing safety checks, and cleaning dishes after gatherings. From a large office with a picture window overlooking a brimming fountain to a shared office space smaller than the master bedroom of our home. From knowing home as a spacious open floor plan to living in tight vertical spaces; from driving anywhere we want to being dependent on public transportation.

> The very things that bring *comfort* can keep us enslaved to the past and unable to move *forward*.

I take solace in the Exodus, from Moses living on a quiet hillside among sheep and family to navigating the hard, nomadic lifestyle endured before reaching the Promised Land. Had Moses foreseen the future, would he have agreed to God's plan? Would he have chosen being perpetually uprooted to wander into the unknown? *Take us back* was the response of the Israelites every time they encountered hardship, defining themselves by what made them feel certain—meat, food, and comfort in familiarity. But the very things that bring comfort can keep us enslaved to the past and unable to move forward. God removes those things for which we rely upon for surety outside of the certainty of his loving presence.

MY GRANDPARENTS PASSED away by the time I gave birth to my daughter, over two decades ago, making the sudden onset of emotions while photographing flowers in the Cotswolds seem slightly misplaced. While surveying a butterscotch patchwork of hills punctuated by hay bales, I hear a small whisper break through the stillness in nature. *I know you miss them. That's why I gave you the Dentons.* A church bell rings in the distance. I cup hands over my face in the realization of being known by God. Pulling a tissue from a coat pocket, I wipe a tear off my cheek as the camera dangles at my hip from the strap resting over my shoulder.

I met Michael and Avril Denton on our first Sunday as disoriented travelers relocating from a small resort community to urban sprawl. Michael bounced up to me at St. Barnabas Church Kensington, holding a stick blooming with tiny pink flowers as a welcome gift. His wife, Avril, stood shyly behind him, wearing wire oval frames and a grin on her face. At that time, Michael didn't know about my love of gardening, healthy addiction to plants, or the sorrow I experienced in leaving well-loved potted friends behind in the United States. That token branch was God's metaphor, a sign that springtime of the heart comes after the barrenness of a winter season. Michael's quirky welcome gift was a kind of wave from God declaring, *I'm here. I see you. I know what you need.* Amid your current uncertainties, what are the signs God is giving you that communicate, *I'm here. I see you. I know what you need?*

Before a morning walk in the Cotswolds with my camera, I woke up in the grand guest room of the Dentons' charming cottage, a spacious place in the house I've overheard them refer to as *Shelly's room* after repeated visits. When they pack up on Sunday and return to London, I stay behind, borrowing their beautiful weekend home for self-imposed writing retreats during the week, making use of the quiet countryside as inspiration for large word counts. Fastidious purveyors of historic chandeliers in Notting Hill, the Dentons are welding metal arms, gilding candle cups, and entertaining notable clientele from faraway places while I am stringing words together in paragraphs.

Weekend stays with my grandparents included Saturday strolls at the Missouri Botanical Garden in St. Louis and cultivating tomatoes and roses alongside my grandfather in the backyard. Horticulture was a focus of weekend activities. And unbeknownst to the Dentons, whenever I'm a guest in their beautiful house, a Saturday outing is planned to a new-to-me garden and nostalgia is unleashed. Grocery bags recycle as temporary containers for Canterbury belles and hollyhocks uprooted from the abundance in their private garden; transported in the trunk, next to suitcases, on the journey back home. Our little walled garden in London blooms with fond seasonal remembrances from times away in their home.

Expressions of love come carefully crafted by our Creator. He knows what makes your heart swoon; what makes you gasp and hold your breath. For me, Love is often revealed in the beauty and details of nature and architecture. Traipsing a historical garden triggers whatever is dormant to come alive within me. For you, it may be carefully crafted words read in a book that become sacred echoes to thoughts. Perhaps restoring old materials into new uses speak of God's healing for your brokenness. Finding a heart-shaped pebble during a walk can translate as a divine love note specifically placed and communicating, *You're not alone, I'm here with you.*

WALKING THE PUBLIC footpath through a farmer's dormant patch of earth, pheasants run wild and mingle in the bushes like chatty women huddling together for gossip, only to scatter in the presence of humans slowly making the pilgrimage back home after a morning jaunt. Dogs run off leash, bounding over hills and trampling through brooks as if they've been freed to participate in a competitive scavenger hunt. As I frame robust bales of hay in the foreground, a house with smoke curling from the chimney in the background uses depth and scale to bring perspective.

When life becomes two-dimensional, flat, and lifeless due to uncertainty, framing your situation from a different angle provides new discovery—from being alone and exiled by your circumstances to being accompanied by God, the author and caretaker of your story. What looks tired, fallow, and unusable in your life is often God's useful preparation for a new season he is planning. Survey your surroundings—crouch down, look up, tilt your head sideways, and capture the scale and depth of God's love. Perspective identifies the intersection of lines falling in pleasant places, even when the lines seem oddly out of place. And like the psalmist, perspective promotes a confident declaration, "Yes, I have a good heritage!" (see Psalm 16:6).

Moses understood the plight of an exile, living as a foreigner in a strange land; what it means to feel other than and yet fully at home. For forty years, he lived a humble existence, working as a shepherd, isolated while tending his father-in-law's flock. It wasn't a stalk of Queen Anne's lace that garnered Moses' attention, but a bush blazing like a torch on the far side of the desert. Curiosity drew him closer to the scene, but the intimacy of God calling, "Moses! Moses!" led to reverence. Moses replied, "*Hineni*," which literally means, "Here I am." He was essentially saying, "Here I am, God, ready and waiting to do your will. Here I am (a peregrini), a partner with you in the eternal covenant between you and your people. How can I fulfill my role more fully?" Like a peregrini, receptive while living simultaneously in the past, present, and future, Moses' response was open and receptive.

Aware of how the past shapes your identity and values, envision a future unhindered by your brokenness. Can you be committed to live as a guest of the world in response to the love of your heavenly Father? Moses was in Midian, on Mount Horeb, translated in Hebrew as "desolation," as the result of fleeing after committing murder. But Moses didn't hide his face in shame for past sins, but rather as a response to God's holiness.

AN INITIAL REACTION to uncertainty can be the fear of God's judgment—what have I done wrong to deserve this? Retreating or "hiding your face" can be a kind of self-protection from all the ways you fear you may be found out. But the more we lean in to listen, what we hear sounds like the certainty of love and the audacity of belief rather than criticism and judgment. God said to Moses, "So now, go. I am sending you to Pharaoh to bring my people the Israelites out of Egypt."

What divine promotion into something new might you be missing because you are afraid of what you might hear? This is what I know to be true: What you hear won't be what you expect, but it will be deeply personal; calling you by name and calling out purpose planned long ago based on his belief in you. What might be the outcome of changing your response from "Why me?" to "Here I am!"

It was only when the comfortable routines of crisscrossing hills and dales with sheep were interrupted that Moses' life began to change, from serving behind the scenes to leading out in the open. Disruptions in life break familiar habits that foster self-sufficiency because we are created to be reliant on God. According to the groundbreaking book *The Power of Habit* by Charles Duhigg, his research tells us that cravings drive our "habit loops."[1] Some of us crave escape or relaxation through the habit of a glass of wine after work. Others crave companionship and have the habit of saying yes to social opportunities as avoidance for being alone. Maybe you crave having the last word and are characterized by the habit of speaking first, before listening in love. Most of us crave certainty and possess the habit of polling friends, researching options, borrowing money, overspending, or using nostalgia as the measuring tool for assigning value in

An initial *reaction*
to uncertainty
can be the fear
of God's *judgment*—
what have I done
wrong to *deserve* this?

the present. Making something happen rather than waiting on God is to create faux peace that is temporal.

We can alternate routines as methodology for dealing with anxiety associated with uncertainty. "For some habits, however, there's one other ingredient that's necessary: belief. One group of researchers at the Alcohol Research Group in California, for instance, noticed a pattern in interviews. Over and over again, alcoholics said the same thing: Identifying cues and choosing new routines is important, but without another ingredient, the new habits never fully took hold. The secret, the alcoholics said, was God."[2]

"For habits to permanently change, people must believe change is feasible. . . . Belief is easier when it occurs within a community."[3] Even if community means one other person. Or in my case, two people, my grandparents, and, later, the Dentons.

Moses is hesitant to believe God has chosen the right person to lead the Israelites out of captivity. "Who am I that I should go to Pharaoh and bring the Israelites out of Egypt?" But God doesn't issue a rational answer for Moses' questions about his ability. Instead, God says, "I will be with you" (Exodus 3:11-12). And then he assigns his brother, Aaron, to be Moses' companion.

INITIALLY, WE CAN feel vulnerable, alone, disappointed, and empty when those things we assign as security are suddenly snatched out from under us. The less we know about the future, the more anxious we become. How can you believe God is working all things together for your good when it looks like he's left the building? Or left you standing alone on a hill in a country not your own? How can an answer to prayer come by way of loss? How might disorientation provide a reorientation toward providence? The answer for your great unknowing is knowing you are not alone; knowing you are deeply loved and fully known by the Almighty. "I will personally go with you, and I will give you rest—everything will be fine for you" (Exodus 33:14 NLT).

If you are someone who looks for the tangible and concrete as signs for safety and security, *I will be with you*, as God's answer for your uncertainty, may feel like walking naked through darkness in a strange place. Rarely is someone eager to surrender the covering of self-reliance in exchange for the risk of wandering into the unknown with the unseen. Finding comfort in familiarity is our normal, knee-jerk reaction when life feels like a giant question mark. But when we use certainty in circumstances as the gauge for our worth and value, that subversive self-reliance can mutate into a prison we choose for ourselves, keeping us from flourishing. Here's the tension in the truth: Uncertainty causes anxiety, provoking us to choose coping mechanisms outside of Christ. But when we look at uncertainty through the lens of being loved by God, what we discern is greater purpose, deeper meaning, and broad perspective. Love asks the most important question we are hesitant to ask ourselves: *What are you relying on to feel at peace in the world?*

Understandably, the uncertainty we experience today is circumstantially different from the Israelites who wandered through the desert for forty years. Moses wasn't a politician; he was a shepherd. His preferred mode of communication wasn't a middle-of-the-night tweet but recounting what he heard God say after times in the Tent of Meeting. Before public opinion, Moses sought God for direction. He might have shown frustration with whining, discontented people, but Moses isn't characterized as reactive. He leads because he loves people, rather than negotiating because he loves winning.

One day Moses said to the Lord, "If it is true that you look favorably on me, let me know your ways so I may understand you more fully and continue to enjoy your favor. And remember that this nation is your very own people. . . . How will anyone know that you look favorably on me—on me and on your people—if you don't go with us? For your presence among us sets your people and me apart from all other people on the earth" (Exodus 33:13–15 NLT).

What makes an anxious society? We want to be different and stand out as unique without the presence of Jesus setting us apart. Realistically, people who are labeled *different* are often set apart as undesirable by the world. Our differences create division as comparison becomes a measuring tool of value and worth. How do you discern the favor of God outside the tangible and concrete of your circumstances? How do you discern God's presence when the headlines declare His seeming silence?

We cannot discern truth from falsity without identifying God's voice in Scripture. We cannot understand who we truly are and why we are here without discerning who God says we are through prayerful conversations. We cannot realize the promises of God without knowing what he has promised to give us. We cannot criticize leadership if we have not sought God's leadership into the future.

Maybe you are blindsided by an unexpected situation that has you echoing Moses, *Who am I?* Who am I to be tasked with leading people, assuming a position of authority, influencing people for the kingdom? Or perhaps you are thinking, *Who am I?* but no one is hearing the conversation you have with yourself on repeat—*Who am I to give an opinion . . . apply for that job . . . lead a small group . . . invite her to coffee . . . speak at that conference . . . ask her out on a date . . . promote my creative work on social media?* How might God's response to Moses—*I will be with you*—be the answer for your uncertainty?

When you are allowed the grace of imperfection—the opportunity to practice without expectation of certainty—doubt cannot gain a stronghold on your confidence. Uncertainty becomes inconsequential when canopied by love and acceptance. When you know you are fully known and deeply loved, freedom in belonging is the outcome.

God said to Moses, "I AM who I AM. This is what you are to say to the Israelites: 'I AM has sent me to you.'" In Hebrew, it's translated as *ehyeh-asher-ehyeh*, meaning *whatever I am, I will be*. He is consistent, unchanging, stable, steady, the opposite of moody or recalcitrant. I AM as the answer for Moses' doubt redirected self-focus toward focus on God's attributes. Knowing that God is always compassionate, always kind, and always loving in response to uncertainty in the world releases us from the fear that God will not come through during chaos and turmoil. We are most safe not when the details of life seem perfectly ordered, but when we are listening for the still, small voice of the I AM in the messy mundane of the everyday.

From an early age we find certainty in attachment to routine—a bedtime story, rote prayer, good-night kiss, glass of water, favorite blanket—as a way of cultivating peace required to fall asleep. I can only imagine that whatever I had grown attached to in the short time my parents were together had been corrupted by their divorce. Whatever security I had grown accustomed to equating with peace and harmony as an American dissolved when we decided to live in England. As a child, a milk shake provided the counterfeit comfort of predictable outcomes. And as an adult, cultural familiarity satiates a hunger for certainty. What relief are you choosing that has become a counterfeit for the Comforter?

Daily decisions, big and small, from what you will eat for dinner to whom you choose to marry, set a course for your life. The people you meet, the places you encounter, and the circumstances you experience all culminate into a story with purpose that has been shaping your life. Sometimes what you assign as random smudges on the pages of your story are divine fingerprints from the hand of the Creator when you take a closer look.

I was wrong about the Queen Anne's lace. It turns out I was photographing Cow Parsley. Same family, different variety in the UK. As an American living among Brits, capturing nuances in the English language requires attentiveness. And God speaks the language of nuance, and discerning his voice comes through fostering friendship with him. While we are seeking common, concrete solutions to assuage anxiety and stress, God is giving us assurances nuanced toward being known and loved by him. Same family, unique relationship. God knows where it is that your faith will be strengthened most and who the people are that will promote your spiritual, mental, and physical growth. He knows the kind of atmosphere that will cause you to thrive at each age and stage of your life. Familiar with your frame, he understands the intricacies involved for flourishing and what leads to veering off the path. The way to clarity is through the complexities of life. Your uncertainty is God's opportunity to grow something uniquely beautiful within you.

Unfortunately, we will never see a divine finger pointing which way to go when encountering a fork in the road. Rarely will someone hear an audible "This is what you need to do next." The peregrinatio journey is a quest of transformation that is continual, rooted in the ancient truth that the depth and scale of God's love bring the clarity of perspective. The journey of a peregrini is only possible when rooted in one's self as Christ's ambassador. We may feel like exiles, stripped of familiarity, living in places where belonging is scarce, among people foreign to God's nature and character, but wandering through uncertainty keeps eyes looking up, outward, and focused. Without darkness, light is indiscernible.

Practice BREAKING HABITS FOR THE WILDERNESS OF BEING STUCK IN FAMILIARITY

What are you in the habit of telling yourself at first light?
E.g., *I'm tired. I'll never get everything done today. I can't do this. This is the day the Lord has made, and I will rejoice in it!*
How do you choose to fill up quietness? E.g., scroll, eat, talk on the phone, post an update on social media, read a magazine, pray, listen, nap.

What are you afraid you might hear if you were to stop and listen?

What does love sound like to you?

How does your inner voice sound when you stop and listen to it? Accusatory? Grateful? Critical/kind? Judgmental? Generous?

What does the voice of God sound like to you?

How have you confused the voice of God with your own voice? How do you know the difference?

What habit is keeping you stuck in the same place and mind-set?

What one person could you ask to keep you accountable as you disrupt unproductive habits? Set a goal to reach out and make a plan.

FIVE

Help Me Decide

Stand at the intersection
of comfort and courage

Your vantage point blindsided
by dark, empty pathways

Pitted pavement leads to
mysterious places

At the street corner of idealism and reality
is the crossroads where beauty awakens

Cross the road wearing sensible shoes
Or go barefoot. Dangle straps
from expectant hands.

Comfort and courage cannot coexist
when walking Home.

SHORTLY AFTER ARRIVING in London, I began seeing new names appear in my inbox. True to form, reserved British readers who had stealthily been following my journey to England waited until I arrived on their home soil to reach out. There were invitations for tea, meeting up for coffee at a cafe, offers for walks along the Thames, and lunches in charming places. Emails were kind, gracious, and discerning about personal preferences based on what they were gleaning from reading my blog.

The letters provided an acute awareness of being known by strangers without my knowing much of anything about the "pen pals." As online readers transformed into face-to-face encounters, the more confident I became in discerning character and intention based on voice in those letters. It turns out, I was right about Elaine.

The first time Elaine reached out, we agreed to meet at a nearby tearoom, a few steps away from the permanent address my family had only just started referring to as *home*. After a brief stint as minimalists living out of suitcases in a house that felt mismatched to our personalities, we moved into what our British friends referred to as a "modern house." Meaning it was less than a hundred years old. Still feeling handicapped by new methods of transportation—after years of driving a Honda minivan on autopilot—tea nearby translated as relief.

Elaine and I drained two pots of English breakfast tea, savored scones slathered with jam and clotted cream, and conversed as if we'd known each other for more than a few hours. When I looked at my watch, I was stunned over how swiftly time had passed. Walking alongside Elaine, down the pavement toward the tube station, we paused at the entrance of my new-to-me terrace house. And she asked why we painted the front door turquoise.

I explained that my friend and fellow author Kristin Schell was pioneering the Turquoise Table[1] movement, mobilizing people in neighborhoods around the world to be "front yard people" by painting picnic tables turquoise and placing them in front yards. The vibrant tables were created as beacons declaring, *I want to know you and be known*. Kristin's mantra mimicked the cry of my heart while in transition among a diverse urban population. But I couldn't exactly pull off a turquoise table at the entrance of my house.

A front yard in London, more commonly referred to as a *garden*, is a rarity. Gardens decorating facades are a familiar charm of the English countryside. But London boasts concrete stoops with pots flanking painted doors and the odd bench under a window surrounded by a wrought-iron fence. A turquoise picnic table in front of a terrace house would look oddly out of place. But a turquoise front door stands as a hinge of prayer and opening of remembrance. *Lord, may we bring your Light and Love to our neighbors and the shopkeepers on our street. May we never forget that it's your heart for the people that brought us to London.*

You might be thinking it's dangerous to meet with a stranger in an unfamiliar locale. I get that, I do. Uncertainty causes us to stay surrounded by the familiar, hoard what we have, and be economical with time and money. But if God is our refuge and place of safety (Psalm 91), how does generosity of spirit translate in contexts that conjure the fear of uncertainty and self-protection? How might being generous with your time open a door for God's glory revealed? If being safe is to be *surrendered to the Almighty for eternal perspective*, how might taking risks—meeting new people, exploring new places, and being open to new opportunities—lead you closer to the heart of God?

At Elaine's invitation, we sat side by side on the low concrete wall growing moss, yards away from my front door, and she led us in a tender prayer, speaking words of blessing over our home as pedestrians walking past brushed our kneecaps. A beautiful beginning to a blooming friendship.

A few months later, I took the train to Richmond for the first time, at the invitation of Elaine, for a wander around her patch of London. On a random weekday, we met among a crowd surrounding a busker belting out tunes at the entrance of the underground. Wearing white-framed sunglasses and a big smile on her face, we embraced in welcome, and then she stood back and looked down at my feet.

"Are those going to be okay for walking today?" she asked, with concern written in arched eyebrows.

She was referring to the pair of tatty black flats on my sockless feet, purchased several years earlier at the Clark outlet store in Myrtle Beach. I knew they weren't a practical choice for walking miles on pavement and navigating through the tall grasses of a public footpath, but they were all I had.

"They'll be fine. These shoes are actually quite comfortable for walking," I explained.

Truthfully, the only pair of trainers (athletic shoes) I owned were in Canada, resting in a plastic bin with a collection of summer shorts and T-shirts at our family cottage. Worn and out of fashion, I made a quick decision to leave the shoes behind the summer before moving to England. But I wasn't fully aware that the radical shift in income when H assumed the position of vicar after being the executive director of a church-planting movement would lead to a long-term parsimonious lifestyle. Perspective on needs versus wants is like the sobering process of repentance. Revelation of need turns the head away from self-sufficiency and back to a dependence upon the all-sufficiency of God. I quickly learned that his mercy and provision are more valuable than the numbers on a paycheck.

Elaine and I conversed while ambling past storefronts boasting the latest fashions and careening under canopies of mature willow, birch, and elm. We strolled beside colorful canoes floating along the canal before reaching the charming destination she had in mind for a cozy lunch. Elaine hadn't a clue Petersham Nurseries was on my bucket list. A gardener's haven, the tucked-away cafe is covered by a pergola of mature vines and decorated with Old World charm. Blooms in vases and succulents in pots adorn distressed painted tables surrounded by mismatched antique chairs. Every nook and cranny are a smorgasbord of color, design, and beauty competing with the menu.

"I'll have the same" was my swift revelation after hearing Elaine order quiche and salad. A smart choice when lunching in England.

Afterward, we shared a slice of cake with a cup of tea and snatched a quick jaunt around the emporium of cultivars for sale. But instead of a plant to spruce up our new but severely neglected walled garden, I carried home something unexpected in a shopping bag.

Retracing the path back to the tube station in Richmond, Elaine and I pass the open doors of a shoe store decorated by signs about a seasonal sale. Casually walking inside, Elaine suggests we mooch around for a minute. Feet, I learn during conversation, carry heft in matters of importance because she's had a long history of difficult issues with her own. Her empathy asks me to survey shelves of shoes and pick out a pair I like. Like my turquoise front door, the pair of shoes I carried home on the tube after a special afternoon out are a prayer and remembrance every time I slip them on. *Lord, may my feet carry me to the places and people where your name will be glorified. Help me to remember that your abundance is my provision when I am focused on what I lack.*

From the time we begin making life decisions, we are prone to focus our energies on getting what it is that we long for but don't yet have. Maybe for you that's finding a life partner: You can't fully dream about the future until you walk down the aisle. Or perhaps you are searching for the right place to live and your life feels as if it's on hold while living in a rental. Whether it's securing a lucrative job, having kids, finding the perfect couch or the right shoes, most of us carry around a mental checklist. And until those empty boxes are ticked with big, bold check marks, what is lacking becomes the emphasis. Over time, mental fixation on whatever it is you lack desensitizes the heart to God's abundance being poured out.

> Over time, mental fixation on whatever it is you *lack* desensitizes the heart to God's *abundance* being poured out.

Desire can quickly mutate into an idol of certainty replacing the certainty of God's love. Lack is often a reorientation pointing us back to the heart of God. Because God already knows what we need.

We don't own a car in London, not only because we can't afford to purchase, park, or insure a car, but because we learn quickly that a car for transport is a want more than a need. The ease of navigation and wealth of public transportation is a wonder in London, but I have never been more aware of needing well-made, comfortable shoes until my world became pedestrian. Almost every pair of shoes I packed in the crate in the U.S. became irrelevant once I opened the boxes in England. And choosing shoes has never been easy for me. Not because I have difficult feet, but because uncertainty coupled with the fear of scarcity becomes a setup for doubting myself.

What if I choose wrong? What if I regret the choice? Will I be able to live with the consequences? What if I change my mind? What if my choice affects someone or something negatively? What if people don't approve of the choice I make?

Ever had one or several of those questions bubble up when standing in the aisle of the grocery store? While sitting in the chair at the hair salon? Holding your hand up in class? Signing up to volunteer or signing a check? Contemplating a move? Hitting Publish on a piece of work? You aren't alone. Moses had a bad case of the what-ifs while he was standing right in front of God.

God selects Moses to lead a momentous change in history for the Israelites and, instead of rejoicing, Moses immediately begins projecting potential negative outcomes. "What if they do not believe me or listen to me and say, 'The Lord did not appear to you'?" God turns a staff into a snake, Moses' hand leprous and back to health in a blink, but those miraculous signs aren't enough to sway Moses away from *what if, what if, what if.* God's litany of backup plans, preferred outcomes, and assurances lead Moses to a surprising conclusion: "I'm out. Get someone else to do it." Uncertainty can leave us frozen and indecisive, but the certainty of God's love releases us into expectancy.

WE CAN HAVE all the assurances from God we need yet allow fear to dictate the process of decision-making. What assurance has God given that isn't enough to calm your fear? What uncertainty do you face that God's presence isn't sure? What more assurance do you need that God's purpose will be fulfilled?

The most significant battles we fight in life are the conflicts waged in the mind. How you think about yourself becomes what you believe about yourself, and what you believe about yourself informs the actions you take in life. For instance, if you think your worth and value are measured by what you produce, then you might believe you are an abysmal failure when the disruptions of life keep you from accomplishment. Ever wake up feeling sick and struggle with inner unrest because you cannot get those things checked off your list?

On the other hand, if you think your purpose in life flows from who you are rather than what you do, you live from the belief that who you are cannot be quantified or calculated. You don't need a paycheck or a product to define your value and worth. A day can simply be called *good* because you awakened with breath and your presence glorifies God.

In digital photography, *noise* is defined as aberrant pixels that are not representing the color or the exposure of the scene correctly. Before the world became digital, visual noise was referred to as grain on a printed picture. A grainy image was the result of darkness in the frame. Spiritually, noise can be defined the same way. Mental noise is an aberrant voice we listen to that is not representing the truth correctly. Whether visual distortion or mental disruption, the way to correct noise is the same: a brighter light source and editing. Pray and remember. When we edit lies by saturating the mind with the light of God's truth, we correct false narratives and images we have about life. Light reveals where perspective has been misplaced. Align your mind with Christ and become the least anxious person in the room.

For me, it's not the big things that lead to paralyzing indecision—moving to London, getting married, having kids—it's the little everyday choices that trip me up. Should I get the blue or yellow sponges? Sneakers or flats? Small or large? Brown or black? Hot or medium spice? High-waisted or low rise? Well, there was never really a doubt in my mind about that one. High, of course! But when it came to the replacement of our worn-out silverware, surprisingly, the noise of self-doubt took me to a dark place.

DURING CHRISTMAS, H and I decide that new cutlery will be our gift to each other because we're comfortable in our marriage and the change was long overdue. When we tell our kids about our gifting plans so they won't think a lack of gifts under the tree is a cause for concern, they respond in sacred echoes that sound something like this: "Thank God! I hate those spoons we've used for our entire existence on the planet!"

We had no idea that while they were scooping Cheerios from a bowl of milk, shoveling spicy chili into their mouths, and savoring chocolate chip ice cream, those spoons were making their eating experiences so unpleasant. They never said a word.

The unprovoked honesty of my children alongside the tarnished tines laid next to pretty plates for dinner parties provided a green light of confirmation that our choice of gift was timely. In February, H, Harrison, and I make a planned pit stop in the Cotswolds on our way home from a trip with friends to Scotland. We stretch our legs by walking into the Robert Welch shop on the High Street in Chipping Camden, a popular English artisan, and peruse the cutlery patterns available for purchase.

Dreaming of shiny new silverware replacing the tired antique set inherited several decades earlier from my great-aunt IO, the sister of my grandpa, we are finally poised to take the plunge. Circling each row of place settings, dawdling over desirable designs, weighing them in our palms, feeling the unique features with our fingertips, we were each imagining how the salad forks and soup spoons might look while flanking our blue and white Wedgwood dishes, purchased on clearance at Marshalls years earlier when we lived in Phoenix.

"So, have you narrowed it down? Which patterns do you like the best?" I pose the question to both of my men. Strongly opinionated and well-researched, normally their feedback speaks loudest, and I tend to acquiesce. Keeping the peace is a high value for me.

But this time, I discerned my opinion held the most sway in the pack. Perhaps what I want in this scenario matters most because I typically own the kitchen, or because my husband is humble, kind, and longs to put a smile on my face. Or because *If Mom isn't happy, no one is happy.* But the weight of responsibility coupled with workers ready to close shop for the evening brought on a case of decision fatigue. A slow processor, smack-dab in the preamble to a panic attack, picking out forks felt more like the death of me than a gift to be cherished for years.

Feelings hijack rational thought and I begin asking myself coaching questions instead of allowing fear to bully me into freezing up. What are the feelings communicating? What about this decision is big, weighty, and important? Why am I feeling fear about something that isn't scary or dangerous? What is the deeper truth my emotions are triggering? What are the lies I might be telling myself right now?

A MEMORY EMERGES. As a little girl accompanying my grandparents to Famous Barr in St. Louis, I am tasked with picking out new shoes. One of several young customers with adults wandering around the cubes of new patent leathers and penny loafers, under the spell of warm, ambient up-lighting making shoes look glamorous and important. What do I want? What do I need? Is it possible to have both in one shoe? And new silverware? These are the questions that haunt me.

As a child, I pick a quirky blue-and-white saddle shoe with a heel that is striped in the same colors; laces are braided blue and white too. Everything about the flamboyant design is unique and completely me, even though I am terribly shy. It's the shoe I really want, but is it the shoe I really need? I'm conflicted and remain silent. Practical is prudent, but choosing prudence can often mean suffocating desire. And if we continually push desire away for the sake of practicality, something God-given slowly dies.

In the Cotswolds, change makes me feel like a child again: unhinged, unsure, and insecure about my ability to choose accurately. Bent over a plethora of cutlery patterns laid out on velvet displays, my hands begin shaking and heart pounding the more I loop around all the beautiful stainless-steel knives, forks, and spoons. How can I choose between so many good options? What if I regret the choice I make every time I sit down at the table to eat a meal? What if my family silently despises my choice?

"Maybe we don't need new silverware after all. I mean, is the stuff we're using really that bad? I don't know, I guess I need more time to think about this," I whisper to H while fiddling with a teaspoon.

"We've been thinking about doing this for months," H retorts, "and, yes, it really is that bad. The silver is wearing off and you already know how the kids hate the spoons. If we don't do this now, when will we be back here?"

Moses could blame self-doubt on insecure beginnings, and I could blame indecision on unstable foundations. It's not that I don't know what I want; it's that I am uncertain about what I need when the fear of scarcity sets in. Because to need is to be vulnerable, and when needs are voiced, humiliation is probable. Early on, I suppressed needs and desires to avoid being burdensome to parents whom I had already equated as being burdened by my presence. I didn't realize, until Elaine generously offered to buy me a pair of suitable shoes, that I still struggle with making needs known.

Silencing desire is a kind of safeguard from disappointment. If I don't say what I need and that need isn't met, then I am the only one who suffers that kind of crushing emptiness. But self-protection can form a subversive prison around your heart. How do you know who and what is safe to let in?

What do you need that you aren't communicating to the people you love? What do you desire that feels scary if you were to admit it aloud to someone? How has self-sufficiency robbed you from experiencing the all-sufficiency of God?

Moses admitted his need and received love in response. "[O LORD,] I have never been eloquent, neither in the past nor since you have spoken to your servant. I am slow of speech and tongue" (Exodus 4:10).

And God responds, not with easy, quick-fix solutions, but with more questions. "And who do you think made the human mouth? And who makes some mute, some deaf, some sighted, some blind? Isn't it I, GOD? So, get going. I'll be right there with you—with your mouth! I'll be right there to teach you what to say" (Exodus 4:11–12 *The Message*).

While standing in the aisle of an upscale artisan shop, I admit my need too. *Lord, I admit that I have never been decisive, neither in the past nor since I have become an adult. I am slow to process what I fear and verbalize what I need without feeling as if that vulnerability might crush me. Help me to remember that your redemption is sure no matter my decision.*

When uncertainty triggers the fear of scarcity, we grasp on to the familiar as comfort. Hoarding is often a first response to forecasts for which we have no control. Whether a hurricane or pandemic, the fear of scarcity has us all running to the store to stock up on things of which we might run out: bread, eggs, and toilet paper. If we were honest, most of us will admit that we long for certainty more than the uncertain new things God has in mind for us. I acquiesced and picked the cutlery pattern H liked best. And I never wore the blue and white shoes from Famous Barr after my grandparents forked out the money. The fear of being too much for my peers kept those quirky shoes parked in the bottom of my closet catching dust bunnies.

"Unmade decisions have the power to either close us up in fear or open us up to love. This is both the burden and the gift of our indecision. We get to choose which one we carry," writes Emily P. Freeman.[2] And each time I carry a plate from the dinner table into the kitchen, and drop a piece of silverware on the floor, the heaviness of indecision is released in love through a prayer and remembrance. *Lord, open my heart to love and release me from the burden of self-doubt. As you provide my daily bread, may I remember your decision to choose me first.*

Indecision over things like shoes and silverware isn't as much about picking perfectly as it is about trusting God with outcomes. Noise from voices in the world distort the way we interpret headlines, and our own mental noise can muffle our ability to be discriminate. Discernment flows from intimacy with God. The way in which we recognize truth from falsity is becoming familiar with the tone and cadence of Truth voiced in Scripture. And the more familiar we are with the voice of Truth, the more capable we become in differentiating godly truth from the truth of the world. During wilderness seasons, discernment is a lifeline leading individuals, communities, and nations to be set apart and different in the world.

> Indecision isn't as much about picking *perfectly* as it is about trusting God with *outcomes.*

Perhaps you feel like a slave to your agenda and what others think about you, or a slave to comparison shackled by unrealistic standards. Maybe you are enslaved by legalism, or the memories of legalism in your childhood that still haunt you.

How has the fear of uncertainty become an enslavement that keeps you from deciding? How have you allowed the fear of scarcity to rob you of the joy in living now? Remembering that you are deeply loved and fully known is your deliverance.

Deuteronomy is a book that could be called "Prayer and Remembrance." It's the fifth book of the Pentateuch and the last chapter of Moses' life. The first time he delivered the law, Moses' audience was being set free from exile. And forty years later, he is addressing the second generation on the cusp of realizing God's promises. As is often the case, children are clueless about the brevity of sacrifices and hardship their ancestors endured to reach the place of abundance.

And like a loving parent, Moses was retelling stories from their history as both a warning and a comfort. Remember when this happened . . . remember when you didn't obey . . . remember when God came through for you . . . remember you will have trouble in this world, but God is bigger than your giants. "Remember how the LORD your God led you through the wilderness for these forty years, *humbling you and testing you to prove your character, and to find out whether or not you would obey his commands.* Yes, he humbled you by letting you go hungry and then feeding you with manna, a food previously unknown to you and your ancestors. He did it to teach you that people do not live by bread alone; rather, we live by every word that comes from the mouth of the LORD" (Deuteronomy 8:2–3 NLT, emphasis added).

In fear, we can miss the obvious—that your uncertainty is God's opportunity to reveal his great love for you. "Your clothing did not wear out on you and your foot did not swell these forty years. Know then in your heart that, as a man disciplines his son, the LORD your God disciplines you. So you shall keep the commandments of the LORD your God by walking in his ways and by fearing him" (Deuteronomy 8:4–6 ESV). Did you get that? It may have taken the Israelites forty years to walk to a place that should've taken a few weeks, but their feet never swelled from overuse.

While I am worried about choosing the right shoe and cutlery, perhaps you are concerned about picking the right neighborhood, school, or church. Or maybe like me, it's not the big stuff that causes you to freeze up, but the little everyday decisions: what to cook for dinner or what outfit to wear to a party. Big and small, decisions are opportunities for drawing nearer to Christ. He cares about what you care about.

MOST OF THE major markers shaping my life have happened during random walks. Big ideas for books, moments of clarity about ministry, discernment catalyzing decisions, loneliness leading to the knowledge of being deeply loved—each revelation came as the result of putting one foot in front of the other, conversing with God, and taking thoughts captive. Eugene Peterson reminds me that "The twelve spent the next three years with Jesus; walking—always walking—along the shores of Lake Galilee, in the hills, and through the villages. When you are walking, especially with others, you tend not to be in a hurry. Conversations are relaxed."[3]

Lace up your walking shoes. It's a simple message read from a new screensaver that appears from Microsoft as I open my computer, culling a full inbox of messages that arrived from readers over the weekend. Sitting at my desk on the third floor, overlooking brick walls, windows, and chimneys, I'm wearing slippers, not walking shoes, but the quote translates as an imaginative romantic gesture to garner my attention; pedestrian when I am assuming a posture of hustle. Behind that simple quote, I hear a faint fatherly whisper, *Pray and remember.*

Practice DISCERNING TRUTH IN THE WILDERNESS OF FALSITY

How has decision fatigue kept you from moving forward?
What decision are you facing now that feels bigger than your faith?

How does the noise in your head contribute to indecision?

What are you telling yourself that isn't true?

How is what you are listening to informing belief?

Take a two-minute pause sometime during the day. Set a timer if you must. Close your eyes and allow swirling thoughts to settle like a snow globe being shaken. Ask God this question: "What am I telling myself that isn't true?" Write down what bubbles to the surface. Then ask this question in prayer: "What do you want to tell me that I'm not hearing right now?"

Remember how God has come through for you in the past. Turn what you discern during that two minutes into a *prayer and remembrance* back to him.

SIX

Practice Presence

When I imagine the eyes
of God looking down
upon the crown of my head,
I wonder
if his eyes well up
with the folly of my sin
or pool from laughter
at childish naïveté.

Will His tears drench my curls
or slide off the
hard exterior of self-reliance?

BARE LEGS STICK to the pleather seat as I squirm in the chair next to my mother. While staring at the brass doorplate engraved *Pastor Bill Cuneio* in black letters, a bare-faced woman wearing stacks of neat gray curls held tightly in place by an armory of bobby pins welcomes us in the doorway. "Brother Bill," I hear her whisper in the hallway, "you have some visitors in your office."

According to my Catholic upbringing, holy men wear collars and albs and stand behind lofty pulpits in churches with stained-glass windows. But Brother Bill wears a three-piece suit, halo of Old Spice, and tube of Brylcreem combed through his thick, dark hair; every strand methodically slicked back into place, revealing each tooth of his plastic pocket comb. Below his shiny porcelain forehead and underneath oversized metal frames are the eyes of my grandfather—kind, loving, attentive. The windows in the entryway are impostors for art glass—opaque, colored, faux plastic like a child's abstract crayon masterpiece—but the windows of Bill Cuneio's soul tell me he is the real thing in a crisp, white-collared shirt.

It was the first time I had darkened the door of an evangelical charismatic church, the first time in church alongside my mother on a weekday. I'm sure Brother Bill discerns desperation by reading our body language during introductory remarks. Mom had a bloody fistfight with her girlfriend, leading to our swift departure from the house at the end of the gravel road. But I feared he was too holy for our brokenness. No doubt Brother Bill would tire of us after our initial connection. Be hospitable and long-suffering in the middle of our crisis, until our neediness became suffocating and unpleasant. But I was mistaken. He appears at our front door holding bags of groceries in both arms with the promise of heat blowing through the floor grates in the winter. He is young and charismatic, and I hear my grandfather's wisdom and comfort coming through a distinct cadence in Brother Bill's voice that is memorable.

Small beginnings from the contemporary condo in St. Louis spiral down to a tiny two-bedroom house with slanting floors in rural Missouri. Our landlady has pink hair, red lips, and facial tributaries so vast and deep, they rival the unnatural oddity of her smoky, masculine voice. The only things she and my mother have in common are smoking Larks, unlucky circumstances, and good taste in furniture and clothing. The beige industrial carpet covering the deferred maintenance of the kitchen floor was a hint to the prevarication of her character.

Tearing open the brown paper wrapper on a stack of graham crackers, my eyes catch movement on the wall beside the refrigerator. Gently pulling two cracker sheets from the package to avoid splitting them, I look up and crumbs scatter over the surface of our dark wood table. The moving object in my peripheral vision, I assess, is a cockroach the size of a small mouse. Slowly taking two methodical steps away from the table, I flip the light switch on, drop the graham crackers, and run barefoot into my bedroom to find a weapon.

From a small crack between the electrical plate and the wall, an army of large black cockroaches squirm out, like soldiers climbing over an obstacle course. Tiptoeing closer, arm lifted, poised and ready, I smack my penny loafer onto the new beige carpet, squashing the enemies one by one, screaming in disgust as cigarette smoke from the living room halos the kitchen. I lose track of counting the dead after reaching fifty.

DRESSES SLOWLY REPLACE flannels on the hangers in my closet, and I no longer depend on friends to pick me up for church on Sunday morning. The most satisfying surprise about our Pentecostal schooling is the revelation that one of my classmates is seated among peers on the pumpkin-colored pews. Karetha never mentioned attending church while walking the halls of Sullivan High with our best friend, Laura, but suddenly the extreme kindness and generosity of her parents during late-night sleepovers begins making sense. Later, I often wondered if her mother was related to the woman who met us at Faith Assembly of God during our initial visit with Brother Bill. Or perhaps they just shared the same hairstylist.

By default, Karetha becomes my tutor in charismatic church etiquette when our spiritual worlds collide. You might as well ask me to strip down on stage when you tell me to raise my hands in church or dance in the pews. The Catholics I grew up with don't do that. I've been comfortable in the confines of my personal space, seated between grandparents and their rosaries. Watching everyone stand in line to receive Communion from the priest is the most vulnerable part of a Mass. Worship at Faith Assembly of God doesn't include kneelers, Communion lines, or keeping discernment to yourself. As an adolescent, I wasn't challenged to explore the uncomfortable place between the limits of my perspective and the mystery of his attributes. I assumed cabernet in the gold cup was commonplace but quickly learn that grape juice is served in plastic thimbles.

"What do we do now?" I whisper to Karetha as we hunker down on our knees, lean into the upholstered pew, faces planted in a posture of prayerful surrender. We're supposed to be praying but she is leaning into me, whispering in my ear, and explaining each part of the service as it unfolds.

"You're making me feel self-conscious about something I've done my whole life without thinking about it," she whispers. "I never realized it would make someone feel uncomfortable."

"What do we do now?" I continue asking moments later, tilting my head sideways from the tent of my own breath, as the crescendo of music gives permission for people to stand again. Slack-jawed, I watch people lift their arms like students exercising in tandem with their instructor, hands waving gently back and forth, young and old heads tilting back, eyes tightly closed, lips shouting and whispering adoration.

"What do I do now?" I ask God, self-conscious and aware of the ephemeral presence of something spiritually different. A few pews to the right, someone speaks in enigmatic low tones, slightly above the collective hum of prayerful voices. Brother Bill stands quietly still behind the pulpit with a peaceful smile on his face. A soporific glow pervades the room, as if I have just showered and dressed after a day of swimming outside on a warm, sunny day. Cheeks are rosy and Son-kissed, and heart is peacefully at rest. I don't want the sun to go down on this new experience.

WHAT DO I do now? It's the self-conscious question we ask in times of uncertainty and prayer of surrender evoking God-consciousness. We're never too old to ask, What do I do now? Moses was eighty and Aaron was eighty-three when they began the Exodus journey, experiencing God as Jehovah as well as the Almighty. Like my first experience as witness to spiritual gifts manifesting, it was only the beginning for Moses when God spoke to him from a burning bush. He saw a staff recoil into a snake, the Nile turn into blood, Egypt teem with frogs, dust transform into an army of gnats, swarms of flies frustrate plans, all livestock wiped out, skin break into oozy boils, hail pelt land, and locusts devour everything that is left. If that wasn't enough, when Pharaoh finally releases the Israelites from slavery, God leads them through the wilderness by a pillar of cloud by day and a pillar of fire by night. In fear of being overtaken by the Egyptians, they scream, What do we do now? And God parts the Red Sea.

Maybe you are riddled with anxiety from stress? Fear being overtaken by too much on your plate? Do you long for people to hold up your arms like the Israelites did for Moses? Is uncertainty making you more self-conscious and less conscious of God? What fear is keeping you from moving deeper into intimacy with him?

Spiritual fathers, mothers, and friends help us discover clarity, squelch fears, extract truth, listen to our lives, and teach us to wait on the Lord when we are prone to prematurely push things along. Who are your helpers? And whom can you help? The faith of Karetha helps me press into the fear of the unknown and find peace on the other side. The belief of Brother Bill challenges my faith in something bigger than circumstances. I accept Jesus

Christ as my Savior for the very first time at the altar of Faith Assembly of God. It only takes the faith and belief of one person to lead someone into change that is life-giving and transformative.

Jethro provides safe retreat and a livelihood for Moses for forty years. The number forty is repeated throughout the Bible 146 times, symbolizing a season of being set apart for testing, trial, or probation. The Israelites wandered for forty years; Moses lived forty years in Egypt and forty years in the desert before he led the Israelites into freedom. He met with God on Mount Sinai for forty days on two separate occasions and sent spies out for forty days, investigating the Promised Land. We have clocks but God has time. What might result if you were to stop, listen, and rest in God for forty minutes once a week? How might that surrender lead to a life-changing experience with God over the next forty days? How might a legacy built on forty years of certainty that you are loved impact future generations?

> We have *clocks* but God has *time*.

IF MOSES WAS in a period of training and testing while living in the desert of Midian, then we can assume Jethro was a worthy coach and mentor. Not only did Jethro celebrate and affirm the accomplishments of Moses, but he wasn't afraid to speak the truth.

> What is this you are doing for the people? Why do you alone sit as judge, while all these people stand round you from morning till evening? . . . . What you are doing is not good. You and these people who come to you will only wear yourselves out. The work is too heavy for you; you cannot handle it alone. Listen now to me and I will give you some advice, and may God be with you.
>
> Exodus 18:14, 17–19

Analyzing those questions from Jethro, I am confident that he was acting as both coach and mentor to Moses. A mentor offers advice based on personal experience, and a coach listens alongside, discerning where God is already at work in an individual's life through open-ended questions. Both are relational experiences in which one person facilitates another to discover their God-given potential. Much of the time, when we ask, *What do I do now?* we are seeking situational clarity, but God longs for you to have sovereign perspective. And we cannot come to clarity alone; we need someone skilled in asking the right questions for breakthrough to happen. We need each other. Coaching is focused on discovery rather than teaching or telling people what to do, because self-discovery leads to ownership of personal changes required to grow. The more we discover, the greater the potential for owning choices that lead to transformation. Jethro listened and posed questions, facilitating healthy leadership in Moses. And being asked the right questions led to a breakthrough in leadership for me too.

ASSUMING I WAS invited to a coach certification course as a consolation of my husband's leadership gifting, I tagged along with H because the location was in warm, sunny California, the hotel room was covered, and having time together without kids was a rarity. Coaching and mentoring are intuitive for my personality and helpful in the role of clergy spouse. Therefore, I could happily endure the coaching classes if shopping and eating food I didn't have to cook were part of the deal. But when I walked into the conference room and began reading name tags of influencers from mega ministries, my deepest fear was brought to the surface: being exposed publicly as incompetent. A scared little girl trapped in the body of a woman who didn't believe she was a leader yet, I didn't feel worthy of being in the room, and I began questioning what I had agreed to in haste.

On the second day of instruction, I awakened in the hotel with a familiar low backache that threatened keeping me in bed rather than seated at a conference table. For me, low back pain is triggered by anxiety, a sign that comes with a warning, *You are taking on something heavy that isn't meant to be yours to hold.* Much to my surprise, when I returned to the venue, I was welcomed by a new comfortable swivel chair, ice pack lying in the seat, and a greeting card signed by everyone on the training course—ministry leaders and corporate execs. Obviously, word about my sore back had traveled fast among a group of empathetic strangers.

During a coffee break, I gently reached forward, attempting to extract a Styrofoam cup from the upturned stack, when one of those leaders intercepted my reach, gently offering help. "What brought on the backache?" he asked, while pressing the lever on a Thermos of hot water, filling the cup on my behalf.

"Oh, this always tends to happen whenever I am doing anything new. My back goes out when I feel overwhelmed or incompetent," I whispered while holding pain in my lower back with both palms.

"That's interesting," he said, making small talk while ripping open a paper envelope holding a tea bag. "Do you remember the first time you felt overwhelmed by something new? Because our physical bodies often revert to the way we first hold fear."

It was as if his question hit rewind on a movie documenting my life, freeze-framing on a childhood memory. "Yes, I do remember," I told him, "but I haven't thought about that in years." What I was too embarrassed to say out loud is that I saw a candid of myself, seated on a bus with a giant teddy bear in the seat next to me.

I was fifteen. It was during the summer before my junior year of high school, and Mom's attendance at Faith Assembly of God was slowly dwindling along with her resolve to drink less wine after dinner. We were about to reach the tipping point in the predictable cycle of making a fresh start, and Tulsa had captured her affection. Moving closer to relatives in her birth state of Oklahoma seemed like a rational place to land after long hours working her fingers to the bone at a shoe factory, making a meager wage and living in a cockroach-infested house. But I became stiff-necked about staying put. Maybe for her, Sullivan, Missouri, lacked opportunity for advancement, but for me, it was roots in intimate community, the place germinating my faith, and where friendships were blooming. At summer's end, she moved to Tulsa, relinquishing my father's forty-dollars-a-week child support check, leaving me in the care of a couple with two small children. I would babysit in exchange for room and board. But a few weeks after I moved my white provincial furniture into their spare bedroom, I became uncomfortable around the man of the house and expressed that fear to my best friend, Laura, in a casual conversation.

A few days later, while sitting in an armchair in their living room, out of the large picture window of the house, I saw Laura's father, a well-respected undertaker in the community, backing his pickup truck to the front door of the house. He was my knight in shining armor, providing rescue and changing the narrative in that short chapter of my story. My new temporary bedroom was in the house of my best friend, attached to Eaton's Funeral Home. Laura and I often traipsed through the casket room back and forth to school. But her generous, hospitable parents became concerned about the legal ramifications of having a child living in their home should something terrible happen. An intuitive response from someone who experiences death on the regular. They asked my mother for custody and she said no.

That's when Aunt Paula, the third sister of four behind my mother, extended an invitation to live with her in a tiny one-bedroom apartment in Broken Arrow, Oklahoma. Leaving my childhood furniture behind, I boarded a Greyhound bus with a one-way ticket in hand. A giant furry teddy bear—a cherished parting gift from peers attending a going-away party thrown

When you become
a *listener* of life
rather than
a *responder* to life,
you break
through *facades*.

at Laura's house the night before—was propped up in the seat beside me.

When was the first time I felt overwhelmed by something new and held fear in my back? I was a scared little girl frozen in the body of a teenager, trying hard to look brave while using a teddy bear as a shield of protection from creepy strangers boarding the bus.

"Our bodies often tell us when there is something unresolved that needs healing," my new friend interjected, sipping coffee from his mug. "What might God be trying to communicate to you through your back going out?"

Unbeknownst to me at the time, this man was organically practicing coaching skills at the snack station. The virtual candid that emerged of the bus and teddy bear led to an epiphany, which led to a breakthrough that led to making choices radically changing the trajectory of my life. I thought I was tagging along on a certification course but ended up being certified to practice one of the most fulfilling privileges of my life: coaching people into clarity that leads to breakthrough and discovery about big-picture purpose. When you become a listener *of* life rather than a responder *to* life, you break through facades of self-protection and discover the real self that God has been protecting since he created you.

JETHRO DELIVERS A wise, alternative plan to release Moses from a burden he wasn't required by God to bear, and "Moses listened to his father-in-law and did everything he said." From the Hebrew name *Yitro*, which was derived from the Hebrew word *yeter*, Jethro is the name meaning *abundance*. When you become grace for someone else, they receive the abundance of God poured out through your life. And when you receive the wisdom and experience of a coach, your life flourishes from the seeds of their sacrificial love. Jethro leaves Moses and returns to

Midian, and the Bible gives us no hint as to whether their paths cross again. A capable coach knows that his role is not to fix or enable but to listen in love for a season and move on.

Like Moses, over the course of our lives, mentors and coaches help us navigate important markers leading to destiny. Many are situational, rooted in a place for a time, while others remain linked to us throughout life. Though I never graduated from Sullivan High School and never returned to the area, my name was included on the student roster for a twenty-five-year reunion due to being tied to the hearts of Laura and Karetha past puberty.

When Laura picked me up at the airport, all the candid memories of our friendship flipped through my mind. Of walking the halls, playing tennis, passing notes, staying up late, talking about boys, and dreaming cross-legged on shag carpet with *Bride* magazine in our laps. From the moment we embrace in the airport terminal, ease in conversation and connection return. But her generous spirit isn't the same as I remember; it's beautifully pronounced, magnified and enhanced by time and experience.

While on a quick tour of her spacious Midwestern house, we walk into the bedroom of her teenage twin girls and stand silently for a moment. "Do you recognize anything familiar?" she asks, with arched eyebrows and a smile on her face.

Inspecting matching quilts, scanning headboards and trinkets on shelves, I reply, "No, actually, I don't."

"The furniture is yours! It was left in my parents' house all those years ago," she admits with nervous, guttural laughter. "I always felt guilty about using it, but I knew you didn't have a way to get it back."

How could I be upset by the legacy of my life living on in the house of the person who saved me? How could I be disappointed if the scaffolding of our friendship could provide usefulness for her own children? I admit, the furniture appeared much smaller and less grand than I remembered, but the big memories associated with the shelves and drawers were redeemed in the bedroom of Laura's children.

After the reunion, I hitch a ride back to the St. Louis airport with Karetha, her parents playing chauffeurs. From the backseat, I listen to the delightful Southern drawl coming from the voice of her mother as the roller coaster at Six Flags blurs past my window. Asking questions from candids of the past, she catches me up on the headlines from Faith Assembly of God. Brother Bill has moved on. But thirty years after I prayed the prayer of salvation, I encounter his voice again and the moment takes my breath away.

THE EVENING SKYLINE in Greensboro, North Carolina, twinkles like fairy dust from the top floor of our Sheraton suite, wooing me like a magician with a swinging clock. Lingering is a luxury I can't afford as a journalist on the hunt for a good story. I can hear the next wave of conversation descending down the hallway. My name tag proclaiming *Clergy Wife* in bold letters lies across my silk blouse, dangling from an elastic necklace. Most people attending the conference where I'm working know me as *H's Wife*. Some know me by my byline. H swears he'll be known as *Shelly's Husband* someday. His confidence in me has never waned since our union.

As an Anglican priest, helping to lead a church planting movement in North America, H speaks to thousands from a platform in a clergy collar, but he's also killer at arranging stemmed glasses on the minibar, pouring peanuts into plastic bowls, and ordering room service. He's an introverted strategic thinker and I'm an extroverted connector. We make a good team in a room mixed with old friends and new acquaintances.

As waves of people enter the suite, chatter heightens noise in the room, making a quiet *tap-tap-tap* on the door indiscernible to anyone but me.

"Welcome," I say while extending my hand to a male stranger standing alone in the hallway.

"Steve Cuneio," he replies, shaking my hand firmly with his well-defined muscular arm, sporting a military haircut and a thin-lipped smile.

The tone of his voice seems familiar, but his face doesn't ring a bell. This is our first introduction, but I suddenly remember his name from a family dinner conversation earlier in the week; a daily download from H about a new chaplain he is endorsing with the Air Force. But it's not just his name that seems familiar; it's the unique intonation of his voice that captures my attention.

"Cuneio. I once had a pastor by that name, but that was a long time ago," I say, pulling my hand away to smooth the waistband of my jeans. Rolling my eyes, I fill up the empty air between us. "I realize that's like meeting someone from Canada and saying, 'Oh, I have an aunt who lives there.'"

"Oh yeah? Where was that, what church?" he inquires, tilting his head to the side and squinting his eyes in curiosity, not put off by my thoughtless rambling.

"A little church in Missouri called Faith Assembly of God. I'm sure you aren't familiar," I say, waving my hand in the air, attempting to push focus away from me in the conversation.

"That's my dad. He pastored that church when I was a kid," he says calmly, placing hands on each hip, smiling.

I step back, hold my breath, and place my left hand over my chest, then lean full body weight forward into the back of a chair for balance, as if I'm standing in a rocking boat on a churning sea, trying to find stability. A piece of my forgotten childhood is bobbing on the surface of our meeting and the room is watching to see if I'm going to reel in our conversation or let him off the hook. *What do I do now?*

"Faith Assembly of God in Sullivan, Missouri?" I throw out another line of questioning for reassurance.

"Yes, that's the one," he affirms, taking the bait.

Conversation lulls to a hush when several notice my swagger next to the chair as if I'm drunk, eyes closed. And the sudden stillness in the room draws H's eyes away from a conversation at the bar and stretching over the crowd. It's apparent all focus in the room has shifted to Steve and me.

"What happened?" H yells out.

I'm feeling like the actress on stage who forgot her next line in the script. *What do I do now?* I wasn't prepared for what transpired after I answered the door. I want to get this right. I need to get this right. My teenage daughter sits front row on the couch where I was just sitting moments before. She hasn't heard this chapter in her mother's story, and I'm not sure I want her listening to it yet.

Steve and I change scenes, from a standing one-act play to sitting down in the audience next to Murielle and longtime friends Terry and Bob. H hands me a drink. I take a few sips, some deep breaths, try to compose myself, but I can't seem to shake the shock of meeting Steve in such an unlikely place. Steve and I continue talking, pulling out virtual candids from the past one at a time, attempting to locate places and people we have in common. My heart slows to a normal pace, but I can't get past the distraction of Steve's voice and the way it mimics the cadence of Brother Bill.

Steve leans in to the arm of the chair. "You know, Dad ended up leaving the ministry, and unfortunately my parents' marriage didn't survive. He's remarried now and very happy. He became a police officer for a while, but I do think he wonders from time to time why God took him to that little church and what was the fruit of his time there."

"Well, maybe I'm the fruit!" I replied with alacrity, renewed and returning to myself again. "Your dad's influence changed my life. He's the reason why I'm a Christian."

Some time later, Steve and I return to the hallway, standing back right where we were introduced providentially. He dials his dad from the mobile phone in his palm. We both smile from ear to ear as Steve relays the crazy story to his dad and then hands me the phone.

"Hello, Bill," I say with some hesitance. Would his voice sound like I remembered it? Would he even remember my mom and me? After all, it was a short season in our history.

"Shelly, it's so good to hear your voice," he replies. Time has changed much for both of us, but his voice sounds the same.

Walking back inside the bustling hotel suite, Murielle and I make eye contact. She smiles while shaking her head. We are seated in the same place with entirely different views of the same circumstance. Just like me and my mother.

PEREGRINATIO IS AN inner prompting in those who set out, a conviction to do whatever it takes without reward, acclaim, mission accomplished, plaque engraved with accolades, or statue erected in memory. It is also communal, not only solitary. A peregrini is ready to go and is led by the Holy Spirit as Helper. But a peregrini is almost always accompanied by a kindred or mentor. The motivation of a peregrini is love that comes from being captivated by the love of God. And when you are loved in community, bravery comes easier. I'm thankful for Brother Bill, Karetha and Laura, Harry Eaton, and Aunt Paula because they inspire others to become peregrinatio pilgrims. Who are the peregrinis in your life? How might a peregrinatio rule of life change your situational uncertainty into holy certitude? How might an impulse to love eradicate fear?

Practice PRESENCE IN THE WILDERNESS OF BEING ALONE

Ask someone new to join you for conversation this week centered around the question "What is challenging you right now?" What is one thing you could tell someone that they don't already know about you?

Who are the people that you've allowed to speak into your life? When was the last time you welcomed vulnerability in conversation?

What is keeping you from finding community?

Who are your helpers?

Whom can you help?

How does the relationship between Jethro and Moses inform your story? How would you characterize their friendship? What are the admirable traits of Jethro that you would like to possess in a mentoring relationship?

What makes a person influential in your life?

Who is influencing how you view life right now (relative, leader, co-worker, child, teacher, etc.)?

How can you practice presence with someone you love this week?

Today, invite the presence of the Holy Spirit to help you navigate the uncertainty in your life. How might that invitation change your perspective and expectancy?

SEVEN

Winning or Whining?

Wonder about the ways of the world
Become wrecklessly heartsick with longing
Wander childlike, in knee-high grass
Extract box turtles tucked into the fence
Become the princess of your imagination
Sit in the windowseat of this beautiful world
Believe you are who God says you are: Beloved

DURING MY SECOND year of college, a breakup with my
first love leads to falling deeper in love with Jesus. Unable to
find a cure to heal my broken heart, by replaying with friends
how our relationship had gone wrong I begin talking to God
through my grief. And an unusual peace results. I long for more
of that. Nibbling on truth, saturating my mind with Scripture,
seeking wisdom from a campus pastor, and sharing faith with
peers in the dorm, I can taste and see God is good even in my
deep disappointment.

Boredom with college lectures ensue. In the summer, I transfer to a private Christian university, which allows me to take

Bible classes without compromising progress toward a Bachelor of Science in Marketing. However, the transfer from a full ride at a state school to full financial responsibility at a private institution not only challenges my bank account, but my faith in God to provide what I need when I need it.

Working double shifts at Pippin's Pie Pantry in Tulsa, I often return to a bustling dorm after curfew, smelling of blueberries with traces of banana cream on my uniform brown T-shirt; crumbs mingling with a wad of bills in the pockets of a wrap-around patchwork skirt. While friends are gathering for concerts and dinners, I serve triangles of quiche and pie, praying for generosity from customers in tips to help pay for tuition. Mornings after those long shifts, I awaken on the bottom bunk for early morning classes with every muscle screaming as if I had just completed a marathon.

Once my third year of study is successfully complete and schedules are segueing into summer, I move out of a high-rise dorm into my mother's new apartment, after Aunt Paula marries Uncle Jim, they sell their house (and my bedroom), and move to a suburb of Chicago. Sharing sweaty elevator rides with friends alongside their parents, carrying boxes and crates of bedding, clothes, and memorabilia to the trunk of my Honda CRX, I realize many had flown into Tulsa from faraway places to help their children move back home for the summer. Mom was at work, twenty minutes away from campus. Used to being unaccompanied or the last to be picked up for most of those important markers during adolescence—field trips, concerts, performances, award ceremonies, tryouts—this time, being alone translates differently, as empowering rather than deflating.

Living as an exile, shifting to different rental houses and apartment complexes for most of my life, immersion into Christian community at college translates as a sanctuary of safety and bedrock of belonging. But as I drive away from campus, the interpolation of newfound peace into old patterns brings on a stomachache, the place where anxiety manifests. What was

I going back to? What would happen to my heart after a few months living away from peers? How can I use time this summer for the good of my future?

Surrounded by the soft blush tones of Mom's new living room furniture, I survey brass legs of the glass coffee table, feeling like a guest in her home, a completely different person. Confidence overshadows the familiar voice of shame, and what seems on paper like an unwise choice in changing universities begins sounding more like wisdom growing me into a responsible adult, a woman who doesn't need a boyfriend or parents to validate her worth. Challenged to choose how my summer might look differently than first assumed, I dial Dad and ask for permission to spend the summer in South Carolina with him. A few days later, I quit my job as a waitress and reload the trunk of the little white car that friends refer to as my "shoe."

Because Mom works as a salesperson at Automobile Clubs of America (AAA), and good Midwesterners are members, I order a TripTik and learn by way of paper road maps highlighted in yellow marker that the journey from Oklahoma to South Carolina is nearly a thousand miles; fourteen hours from door to door. A newbie on making cross-country road trips, practicality is my safety net. I divide the driving into two days.

At the time, mobile phones, Google maps, and GPS aren't even a thought yet. Journey playing from the stereo, snacks, and a trusty flip-chart map are my companions. Pulling away from the apartment complex, sweaty hands grip the steering wheel as I watch Mom's image, waving from the sidewalk, grow smaller in the rearview mirror. Body is trembling but soul is soaring. I am spending the summer as a peregrini, living in a different place with a long list of unknowns still looming—securing a summer job, paying an upcoming tuition bill, finding community in a new place. As I pull onto the interstate, push into fifth gear, and set the cruise control, I feel brave and adventurous, as if I am experiencing what it means to be an adult in the hands of God for the very first time. I imagine Moses must've felt some of those same emotions as he accepted the challenge to lead the Israelites out of captivity and begin the journey toward Canaan.

Leaving the in-laws' land and sheep, Moses packs his family onto donkeys and begins the trek, clutching a staff rather than a TripTik. Intersecting with his brother Aaron in the desert, they embrace with a kiss and Moses shares everything that has transpired during their separation—all the things God declares he is to say and the miraculous signs provoking their clandestine meeting. Afterward, "Moses and Aaron brought together all the elders of the Israelites, and Aaron told them everything the LORD had said to Moses. He also performed the signs before the people, and they believed. And when they heard that the LORD was concerned about them and had seen their misery, they bowed down and worshiped" (Exodus 4:29-31).

There isn't a person on the planet who does not long to be seen and desire to be known. I longed to be seen by my father as the woman I'd become; to be known by him as more than the daughter he left behind after a divorce, more than a guest in his home for one week of the year. For the Israelites, the longing to be seen and desire to be known were fulfilled when Moses and Aaron arrived on the scene. And they responded by bowing in worship to God, releasing unfathomable joy and thankfulness, perhaps feeling as if they were adults in the hands of a good God again.

We live in the tension between hope in the new things God is releasing us into and the fear that he won't come through in the way we hope he will. Assume your transition will be ordered like a TripTik—predictable, calm, safe, and secure, without moody drivers, traffic jams, or detours—and you are primed for some possible disappointment. Unless you translate unforeseen roadblocks and delays as an opportunity to know God and be known by him.

Without incident, I arrive on the driveway of my father's two-story home, nestled under tall pines on a cul-de-sac in Sugar

Creek, a popular middle-class neighborhood boasting painted shutters and well-manicured lawns. I inhale the manly scent of Dad's aftershave in the morning, notice his well-manicured hands, and admire the wealth of button-down starched shirts left on the screened porch by the dry-cleaning service, transferred to the closet I'm borrowing in the guest room.

For several months, I use a fresh towel for showers every morning; join tennis lessons alongside my half brother, Sean; lounge at the neighborhood pool; shop at department stores with Carol, my stepmom; work as a salesperson at Casual Corner; and endure long days of data entry at a textile mill. Dinner out is a generous gift from my parents, not a choice that I will later be made to regret due to the cost of my meal. Experiencing the luxury of summer in the South for the first time, this, I think, is how real people are meant to live. But deep inside, the message I hear is, "You're an outsider, living as a guest in the world, an exile rather than a daughter." I can almost hear a faint whisper from Moses—*me too*—while he tends sheep that aren't his own in a place that is foreign to his roots, and afterward, when he arrives in Egypt without a home, and begins the long journey toward the Promised Land.

IN PSALM 90, Moses begins, "LORD, you have been our dwelling place throughout all generations. Before the mountains were born or you brought forth the whole world, from everlasting to everlasting you are God." *You have been our dwelling place* written by a man without a country, a fugitive from Egypt leading the Israelites, who are also without a place to call home. Together, living as sojourners in the tension of the in-between, the place of uncertainty, they discover that a man's dwelling is not a place but a Person. It is in God that we find safety, security, and peace that surpasses circumstances. From everlasting to everlasting, Israel's dwelling place is God, and God is eternal. Therefore,

Israel has a dwelling place that is certain and constant. And so do I. But it takes a while for me to come around to that truth.

When it's time to reenter classes and retrace the trek back to Oklahoma, the difference between the price of tuition and the amount in my bank account add up to more than a couple of paychecks from two part-time jobs. And I begin lamenting on the phone to faraway friends with whom I am anticipating an imminent reunion. Fearing a return to the cocoon of belonging might be just out of reach. What will I do if I can't afford to finish a degree? Where will I live? Why did God allow summer spent in a foreign place if the result is living aimless afterward?

Lament, unlike the sulky, ill-tempered mood of whining, is a passionate expression of grief; sorrow expressing regret or disappointment about something. Both lament and whining are familiar responses to uncertainty and nuanced by belief. To lament is to be disappointed yet hopeful, repentant considering God's goodness. But when we whine, we are not just talking to the air; we are grumbling against God. Whining is evidence of unbelief, lack of belief that you are loved. The Exodus story reveals that whining makes God angry while lament as written by the psalmist stirs up empathy and compassion from God's heart as a response.

Further into Psalm 90, searching for the certainty of his significance, Moses prays, "We are consumed by your anger and terrified by your indignation. You have set our iniquities before you, our secret sins in the light of your presence. All our days pass away under your wrath; we finish our years with a moan. Our days may come to seventy years, or eighty, if our strength endures; yet the best of them are but trouble and sorrow, for they quickly pass, and we fly away. If only we knew the power of your anger! Your wrath is as great as the fear that is your due. Teach us to number our days, that we may gain a heart of wisdom" (vv. 7-12).

My days are numbered, and I desire wisdom about how to navigate this season of coming into adulthood and making responsible choices. Am I really wanted? Am I truly seen? Am I known? And loved for who I truly am? What does all this mean? These are the questions at the core of our humanity and questions that challenge what we believe while socked in by the cloud of unknowing. Questions must've plagued the Israelites when things got worse before they got better, before they were released from captivity into freedom.

If Moses and Aaron had assumed everything God said would fall magically into place, like turning the pages on a paper flip-chart map—*turn here, take that on-ramp, tell Pharaoh what I want him to do next*—imagine how confounding Pharaoh's willful response must've been. Let's just say, Pharaoh was not on the same page with Moses and Aaron. Transitions are rife with awkward, uncomfortable, and offensive details that make the promise of a new season a mockery of hope. Lament in the Psalms reminds us that present situations can look bleak before the future becomes clear. "Relent, Lord! How long will it be? Have compassion on your servants."

Instead of releasing the Israelites, Pharaoh refuses to provide what is within his reach and influence, creating undue hardship for them. Withholding straw needed to make bricks made the job more strenuous while the quota of bricks stayed the same. Pharaoh assumed that if the Israelites were consumed by work, they wouldn't have the time to listen to the truth. And perhaps we are still living under the harsh taskmaster of an Egyptian mind-set, consumed by work with little time for discerning truth from noise.

Overexposure is defined as too much light shed on the topic. In photography, so much light we can't discern the whereabouts of the subject matter. Spiritually speaking, excessive media coverage headlining a wealth of bad news makes it difficult to discern God's presence. And overexposure to bad news often leads to apathy. Like the Israelites, we begin to paint the future through the lens of what we don't have.

"When they left Pharaoh, they found Moses and Aaron waiting to meet them, and they said, 'May the LORD look upon you and judge you! You have made us obnoxious to Pharaoh and his officials and have put a sword in their hand to kill us" (Exodus 5:20-21). Ouch. If that isn't a blow to the ego, I'm not sure what is. One minute the Israelites are bowing in worship, and the next minute they are spitting on the sandals of Moses and Aaron. Moses' hope was drowned in the selfishness of Pharaoh's stubbornness.

Moses was being seen and known, but not in the way he might've anticipated. He implores, "Why have you brought trouble on this people? Is this why you sent me? Ever since I went to Pharaoh to speak in your name, he has brought trouble upon this people, and you have not rescued your people at all" (Exodus 5:22-23).

Why? It's often our first response when life isn't mapping out the way we envision. *Why aren't you providing what I need to resume my education?* It was my recurring lament as warm, sunny days in the South shifted into autumn. And decades later, while living in South Carolina, as summer shifted into autumn and autumn fell into winter, my lament was similar. *Why did you lead us to leave a job when fulfilling this role in London is continually delayed? Did you tell us to go so we could be mocked by the people we lead? Ever since we agreed to do what you asked, things have gone wrong. There are no signs you are releasing us at all!*

WHEN I WALK into the living room from my office, H's expression tells me something is awry. He explains how a "little" problem with the steering wheel on Murielle's car turned out to be a $2,300 repair, according to our trusted mechanic. We had just sold her dated Mercedes to a kind woman from New Hampshire over the phone for $2,500, ticking that sale off a long list of to-dos before moving to London. The day before receiving the unwelcome news about the car repair is my birthday. We make a plan to celebrate differently, with breakfast at a local diner. Though my kids have eaten at the popular haunt many times, I had never enjoyed that luxury in all the years we made Pawleys Island home. Checking that off the bucket list before moving away from the area seemed a good option. But mysteriously, the key to Murielle's car went missing while we were seated at the table. H immediately ordered a key to be made for the new owner and the bill for the replacement was $250. Turns out, the selling price was nearly the exact amount needed to make the repair and provide a new spare key. Paying someone to take the car off our hands wasn't what we had envisioned, but we were thankful.

On a sunny Monday morning in Pawleys Island, sitting on Murielle's unmade bed strewn with a menagerie of keepsakes and packing paper, I am helping her sort through years of nostalgia and packing a few boxes for the storage space. It's the day we anticipate receiving more news from London with a possible timeline. But after a chain of unwanted events, I'm emptied of emotional capacity and fear how I might react to another response of *no, not yet.* When the anticipated response from St. Barnabas finally arrives just as they say it will, that fear becomes my reality. A message from Tim saying, "Wait a little longer." H becomes my Moses and I take the posture of the Israelites, railing at him about things getting worse.

"This isn't right, they cannot expect for us to continue putting our lives on hold indefinitely. I'm not going to wait any longer." Running out of Murielle's room into our bedroom, adulting by throwing a tantrum, lopping pillows at the wall, outraged at God, and ranting, "Are you mean-spirited? Why would you allow this to happen?"

Of course, the things we rage about are not out of God's reach—money to pay bills, education for our children, selling a house, finding a place to live, vocation, purpose to wake up to—but they seem too big when the focus becomes projecting outcomes rather than projecting the love of God into our unknowns. Because He never seems to act within our timetable, self-reliance wins. At a time when I'm challenged to experience the spaciousness of God's love, I instead choose imprisonment, confined by fear. The result? For the first time in my life, I begin questioning what I believe. Maybe you've been there too?

Tantrum settles in a dim bedroom and I pick up a book by Brennan Manning lying on the chaise next to me, and it flutters open on my lap. Looking down and glancing at the pages, the light peeking through slats in the shutters illuminates a poignant quote. "To be grateful for an unanswered prayer, to give thanks in a state of interior desolation, to trust in the love of God in the face of the marvels, cruel circumstances, obscenities and commonplaces of life is to whisper a doxology in darkness."[1] My spirit lifts and tears fall off my chin. I want a map for assurance, and God is longing for me to know the assurance of his love.

Comfort comes in words penned long ago by a respected author, and when I was discovering my identity as a college student, assurance comes in words penned by a distant grand-father in a birthday card. A card received at my dad's address in South Carolina before driving back to Oklahoma. Inside the card is a check for the difference needed to pay tuition. Rescue comes from the grandfather I barely know and hadn't heard from in years. And God continues reassuring Moses too. "I am God. I appeared to Abraham, Isaac, and Jacob as The Strong God, but by my name God [I-Am-Present] was not known to them."

The expressions "to know the name of Jehovah" or simply "to know Jehovah" frequently means more than a mere awareness of his name and existence. Rather, "to know" (from the Hebrew word *yada*) often means to *learn by experience*. Perhaps, learning through the experience of *waiting for his presence to be revealed in our circumstances*.

If we name something we want—happily married parents, job security, devoted love, entrance into higher education, pro-motion, pregnancy, flourishing health—but don't obtain what we long for, the result is heartbreak. Envision a future, either near or distant, and rather than fulfillment, a lengthy waiting period ensues. That kind of wait provokes the same physiological response as a broken heart. If what we long for remains only in our imagination and outside of our grasp, we can leap to this wrong conclusion: I've been forgotten, overlooked, or deemed unworthy of love by the One who gave me life and knows me best.

Research reveals that when we experience physical pain from being injured, the angular cingulate cortex (ACC) is stimulated, and surprisingly, the same region of the brain is activated when we experience loss and emotional pain. The ACC appears to play a role in a wide variety of autonomic functions, such as regulating blood pressure and heart rate, but it is also involved in certain higher-level functions, such as reward anticipation, decision-making, impulse control, and emotion. Because the way we process emotional and physical pain is similar, it's not outlandish to say that waiting on God to act on your behalf can feel like having your heart ripped out.

At the same time, the end of a waiting period can often translate as God's favor and lovingkindness, like spring suddenly bursting with color on a sullen winter landscape. We experience the same range of feelings when a wait is over and when we learn that we are deeply loved. But the longer hope is deferred, the more we are prone to doubt, and faith depletes. We begin second-guessing if we ever knew God in the first place. Intellectually, we know that we are seen and known by God, but in the throes of heartbreak, we tell ourselves the opposite. And how we choose to wait inevitably determines where we end up.

Courage comes from the Latin word *cor*, meaning "heart." And courage is often (heart) broken when waiting becomes more than a temporary delay or postponement. Often, waiting becomes an inward exploration on all the ways you don't measure up. Self-assurance is used for navigating the uncomfortable unknowns inherent in waiting periods, but peregrinatio challenges us to explore another way.

Courage from a heart that waits on God is courage that overcomes heartbreak by wandering *into* true Love. While the world uses platform as affirmation of worth, we live in the paradox of loneliness and isolation becoming chronic maladies common to humanity. The mind-set of a peregrini prevents an inward journey from becoming a lonesome interior self-exploration and instead invites a way of approaching life that leads to belonging and being known in relationships. While we are prone to associate waiting as stagnation or being stuck in some dreary, unwanted place, waiting as a peregrini turns times of uncertainty into an active adventure.

Merriam-Webster tells us that the synonyms for *waiting* include *delayed, deterred, postponed, time wasted, on hold,* and *held up.* But this is how God longs for us to wait with him: anticipate, expect, linger, sojourn, and stick around—all antonyms for waiting, according to the same book. Often, the way in which we view waiting is in opposition to God's viewpoint. Instead of feeling held up to fulfill purpose, what if we began to see waiting as an opportunity to experience God's presence leading us on an unexplored path? Lament ushers in a change of perspective, from time as wasted to time for anticipating God's creative imagination for solutions you didn't expect. Successfully navigating unexpected detours in the journey of life is to maintain a curious posture on the mysterious ways of God. A pilgrim sent out versus a sentence to be endured.

Research reveals that when our time is occupied versus unoccupied, waits are perceived as shorter. And when waits are explained versus unexplained, we are more patient. When we understand the reasons for delays, we are more tolerant. For instance, when a pilot alerts passengers to air traffic, when a doctor informs a patient on length of time for test results, when status boards on overground platforms and countdown clocks in tube stations detail when the next train is coming, the result is comfort, maintaining inner peace. Disney has mastered the queue

While we are prone
to associate waiting
as *stagnation*
or being stuck . . .
waiting as a peregrini
turns times
of uncertainty into
an active *adventure*.

for rides by overestimating wait times, meaning we're happy when the wait time is shorter than anticipated. Anxiety increases when you cannot see or monitor wait times. Uncertainty eats us alive, but unfair waits feel longer to us than equitable waits. We are willing to wait longer if we believe that the process is valuable somehow.

"A long and unpleasant wait can damage a customer's view of a brand, cause people to leave a line or not enter it in the first place or discourage them from coming back to the store entirely," writes Ana Swanson in the *Washington Post*.[2]

Spiritually, a long, unpleasant wait on something deeply meaningful can damage a person's view of God, causing people to leave church or not enter in the first place. Waiting can discourage people from coming back to faith entirely, or bring them back to faith, depending on the viewpoint.

Companies use several strategies of distraction when people wait—mirrors, televisions in waiting rooms, reading materials. The data shows that when we are distracted by looking at ourselves in mirrors, it makes waiting less painful. And the greatest tool for distraction is held in our palms on the daily. But all those distractions we choose are temporary counterfeits for Peace that lasts and sustains. If we aren't at peace internally, the externals are superfluous—bricks and straw.

Esther De Waal teaches us that the peregrinatio journey is only possible in finding our roots, "that if one is rooted, at home in one's self, in the place in which one finds oneself, is one able to move forward, to open new boundaries, both exterior and interior, in other words, to embark on a life of continual and never-ending conversion, transformation."[3]

Contentment and certitude are not the same thing. We can experience contentment while waiting to see how our life is going to turn out, but waiting for certitude keeps us from making the cross-country journey into the unknown and celebrating markers of life. Wait for the Lord; be strong and let your heart take courage; wait for the Lord! (Psalm 27:14).

Practice LAMENT IN THE WILDERNESS OF DISAPPOINTMENT

What are you overexposed to right now?

In what ways is overexposure to social media creating apathy in you?

How would you describe your response to disappointment? Are you characterized by lament or whining?

How does the nuance in the meaning of lament and whine change your perspective?

What are you waiting for right now?

How is the absence of what you long for creating new space in your heart? Closing down places in your heart?

Create a new narrative in your current uncertainty by declaring your fears in the voice of love, e.g., *Uncertainty is making me afraid of the future. Ten thousand uncertainties will fall at my side because God is my certainty.*

Write a prayer of lament as a response to the heaviness/disappointment/uncertainty on your heart.

EIGHT

Beholding Beauty for the Big Picture

Love is the soft palms of your hands
molding mine as we meander
crowded streets, calm greens.
Hearts beat in belief. In us.

Love is not a day set apart only by
greeting cards and lacy garments,
but the daily dust of our making
and unmaking.

Beloved,
every day I wake up next to you.

THE INTIMACIES THAT shape us are most often vulnerabilities
we struggle to fully comprehend. But faith recalibrates eyes to
beauty, opens the aperture of understanding, and gives hope a
name. Looking back, hope is best named as an aroma, like a
landmark is to defining a place.

Lying on my back, memorizing the popcorn ceiling from my bedroom mattress, a small stuffed dog sits on my stomach. Six-year-old fingers flap the furry ears on a nearly threadbare body, yellowing in places. One golden eye with black spokes chipped slightly at an angle makes the toy an acceptable character in imaginary stories of trips to the hospital. "It's okay," I whisper. "I'll protect you."

After my parents' divorce and my father's remarriage, my stuffed animals and dolls were my closest confidants, intimate companions bearing the weight of my grief wrapped around them like a mule's yolk. My feather pillow, soaked with tears, wooed me to sleep as I prayed for my mother's contentment.

There was evidence God was hearing my prayers, not by a change in our circumstances, but in fragments of hope extended like a life raft, when despair threatened to drown the limits of my young perspective. The smell of fresh-cut grass trailing through spring's open window. A gentle breeze blowing the curtains of my bedroom like skirts gracefully twirling on the dance floor. Sun casting ambient light over shelves of books and trinkets, making them new all over again. Awakening from a nap to the fragrance of lemon Pledge—all hints of longing for a clean slate, a fresh start, through the strokes of a dust cloth over wood. These scents still remind me of hope.

On many days during young adulthood, despondency led to thoughts about taking my own life, though I knew I would never actually go through with it. Perhaps, if you were honest, you might admit to a fleeting moment or recurring thought of ending it all too. A time when you couldn't bear the difference between life as you know it and the image you envision. The contrast of reality and dream so vivid, pulling a spoon to your lips morphs into an unbearable task.

But then again, maybe you don't carry the burden of the unkindness of not knowing how to love yourself, like so many of us do. I know, it feels more comfortable to earn love, but grace doesn't require work or rules. It's available for your acceptance;

reception without checklists or hoops to jump through. You are loved for who you are, not for what you know, not for what you do. We understand this, but we are slow to believe it.

I've heard stories of those looking for the nearest window ledge, bridge . . . and worse. Read the statistics about boys versus girls—for every one hundred females between ages fifteen and nineteen who commit suicide, there are 549 males.[1] It's startling, isn't it? How are we raising a generation of kids unable to truly love themselves? What kind of culture are we cultivating that loneliness is now an epidemic?

It feels more comfortable to earn love, but grace doesn't require work or rules. It's available for your acceptance.

I've also heard stories about plans with a ledge or a bottle of pills being providentially thwarted. In most cases, it's come from a simple text, a phone call, someone stopping to ask where the Coke machines are in the building, a middle-of-the-night cry from a child's bedroom. All interruptions with the message: *I need you; you matter to me.*

You know why I haven't given up and quit? I believe in hope. And hope isn't a birthright; it's learned through adversity. Despair means "to live apart from hope," meaning hope is essential for life. Without hope, the soul wilts. You can conquer despair, not by making sense of uncertainty but believing that hope for your future is certain. Not trying harder but surrendering to the certainty of God's love.

For me, the smells of fresh-cut grass, burnt marshmallows, and Tide on warm sheets all conjure familiarity, fond memories, and the faithful presence of God. "May he be like rain that falls on the mown grass, like showers that water the earth!" (Psalm 72:6 ESV). Those scents are absent as we make a home in urban London. But lack of familiarity is a reminder that my expectations about life aren't what matter, but what life expects from me matters most. While the Polaroid details of childhood memories seem faded and less significant when edited by time, as a collection, they tell a story of the intimate friendship of God. Familiar scents escort us into the past and help identify the scent of Christ in the panorama of a seemingly senseless world. Beauty is a reorientation from the fear of uncertainty to the certainty of being fully known and deeply loved. "To participate in beauty is to come into the presence of the Holy. It is we who exile ourselves from God," writes Jonathan Edwards.[2]

When Moses met with God in a cloud on Mount Sinai for forty days, one of the items on God's list to discuss were the names of the architect and builder of the temple.

> I have chosen Bezalel son of Uri, the son of Hur of the tribe of Judah, and I have filled him with the Spirit of God, with wisdom, with understanding, with knowledge and with all kinds of skills—to make artistic designs for work in gold, silver and bronze, to cut and set stones, to work in wood, and to engage in all kinds of crafts. Moreover, I have appointed Oholiab son of Ahisamak, of the tribe of Dan, to help him.
>
> Exodus 31:2–6

In Hebrew, *Bezalel* means "in the shadow of God" and *Oholiab* means "tent of the Father." Two men handpicked, nurtured, trained, and named to build the structure inhabited by the holiness of God are simultaneously being shadowed by his presence as they work. Being under the shadow of God's "hand" is to be protected, nurtured, and trained as a father uses his hand to guide the hand of his inexperienced son. And we are shadowed by the hand of God too. "The LORD is your shade on your right hand" (Psalm 121:5 ESV). "The LORD called me from the womb, from the body of my mother he named my name. He made my mouth like a sharp sword; *in the shadow of his hand* he hid me; he made me a polished arrow; in his quiver he hid me away" (Isaiah 49:1–2 ESV, emphasis added).

While the Israelites were exiled without a place to call home for five hundred years, God created permanence through the details of the Temple. "Make the Tabernacle from ten curtains of finely woven linen. Decorate the curtains with blue, purple, and scarlet thread and with skillfully embroidered cherubim. These ten curtains must be exactly the same size" (Exodus 26:1–2 NLT). Gold clasps, goat hair cloth, tanned ram skins, acacia wood, silver bases, bronze ash bucket and shovel, oil of pressed olives for light, two onyx stones engraved with names—beauty is in the intricacies of details, and the specifics are God's way of saying, "I'm here."

Primary beauty is God himself, which means beauty exists only because God exists. Therefore, the harmony, symmetry, and order in creation reflect the nature and character of God. The beauty we experience in creation is secondary to the beauty of God; only beautiful because God made it so. As Christians, when we look at the cross and think *That's beautiful,* our soul is seeing what the world cannot visualize.

On a random Monday, I stumble upon a perfectly manicured garden in London and halt my pace to photograph the beauty, capturing a small glimpse in the panorama that is the Beautiful One. To be found dumbstruck by beauty and awestruck by creation is to be struck by the love of God and rendered speechless. When was the last time you were thunderstruck by the presence of God, overwhelmed by his power rumbling quietly in your midst? For me, that experience took place unexpectedly on a Saturday morning walk to Notting Hill and later in Tuscany.

BEFORE OTHERS IN the house stir from sleep, before the predictable truck barrels over speed bumps on our quiet street, before I roll out of bed and tiptoe downstairs, avoiding places in the stairs that creak, I lie still in bed looking at the smooth, white ceiling and rehearse plans for the day. Once I have stretched my way out from under the sheets, I lean against the downstairs window with a cup of tea steeping in hand. Look past a binocular view of water droplets hanging on the sash and survey impatiens and begonias growing tall and vibrant in the small beds of our walled garden. The outdoor wooden table is soaked from gray to smoke. But the weather forecast predicts a round flaming sun by ten in the morning. *Well, we have some time then,* I think.

A jaunt to the Notting Hill market with girlfriends was set in the diary weeks ago. Faithful to the forecast, sky transforms from dusty shadow to bright cerulean. Once poetry books and Bible are closed, spines placed on shelves and breakfast dishes washed, I lace up white trainers and scurry out the door, carrying a satchel of reusable bags. Ambling past a menagerie of people and pets loitering on pavement, small cafe tables are strewn with newspapers, porcelain cups, and crumbs left as evidence of flaky croissant breakfasts. Crossing over vacant train tracks gleaming in the sun, through a pedestrian crosswalk and up a hill, I walk past Simon Cowell's grand house and intersect with Mila, a friend standing at the entrance of Holland Park, the halfway point for both of us. I have grown to interpret her Russian accent as a sign of God's faithfulness. After all, I prayed for years to live in London, an urban city where diversity and beauty flourish.

"Do you miss home?" I ask as we set navigation on phones and whiz our way past the pristine white facades on millionaire's row in West Kensington.

"I don't have enough time to remember how missing someone feels," she says, smiling.

Her stories of single parenting describe narrow passages for presence with friends, reminding me of how it feels to be the child of a single working mother again. Raised in the tension of passion for work and responsibility in the everyday mundane, empathy erupts. How do you say no to so many good things? How do you rest when others depend upon your ability to keep the flow of life moving?

Turning the corner onto Newcombe, brisk, long strides slow down to small, even steps around white tents displaying crates of vegetables, fruit, jars of jam, potted herbs, and cartons of eggs. Our mutual friend Joy, who organized the morning for us, waves from a distance.

"You have to smell these," Joy regales, while pulling a bunch of pale pink roses from the floral feast soaking in metal buckets, raising blooms up to our nostrils. "Pick out another bouquet, I'm splitting them between the two of you. It's my treat."

"Oh, my goodness, wait a minute," I interject. "I want to take a photo. The petals are so soft, fragrant, and lush. They remind me of the roses growing in my grandparents' garden when I was a child."

From the satchel, I extract my phone and discover the charge has plummeted to zero. My heart wilts as my friends pull stems of flowers from the water. There will be no photos taken of the beauty I'm experiencing. No sharing the wealth of color and texture with friends on social media. No documentation of the sun slanting, creating shadows over freshly picked produce. Before disappointment sets in, stealing the joy in our gathering, I hear a subtle whisper from God that changes my mood. *Pay attention to what you see and inhale the fragrance of the roses because this beauty you are experiencing is just between us. Memorize the moment if you must. I want you to become intimately acquainted with hiddenness.*

UNSEEN, YOU AND I were dreamed up and created. In the darkness of the womb, the beauty of your beating heart was only seen by the Beautiful One. And as we grow into the people God envisions, beauty awakens the incarnation of his presence. In a series of mental Polaroids, I capture a bunch of freshly picked pink roses procured by a friend, tiny white potatoes and fragrant strawberries tucked into my bag—I see how the seeds of our lives are scattered, take root, and blossom into a beautiful panorama of story, the arc revealing God's faithfulness. We can taste, smell, touch, and see that the Lord is good.

The Polaroid is an instant camera and an overarching word used to describe a type of photography using self-developing film to create a chemically developed print immediately. Choosing a Polaroid isn't about quality or clarity as much as capturing a moment and recounting it swiftly. Place *self* in front of most anything and it becomes a lesser version of the real. In photography, self-developing forces what is intended as a slower process into an instant, tangible memento. In real life, self-development is taking steps to better yourself by learning new skills, developing talents, or overcoming bad habits that allow someone to realize dreams and aspirations. And while all those things are worthy, helpful endeavors, focusing on yourself without God guiding the process of your development results in distorted identity. Esteem the self-made man, "but when they measure themselves by one another and compare themselves with one another, they are without understanding" (2 Corinthians 10:12 ESV). Your potential blooms into a beautiful identity when you first believe you are made in the image of God.

What if we replaced all words beginning in *self* with *God*? Following the example of nameless Irish saints who left a legacy of being less self-absorbed and more absorbed with God in the adventure that is life. Can we change our knee-jerk reactions toward self-reliance in times of uncertainty to become a people fully reliant on God in the unknowns? What if we become less self-conscious and known as selfless people; more conscious of God's presence than our current selfie culture. The journey of peregrinatio is characterized not by perfectly scripted outcomes but in finding peace in the disruptions of life.

My empty satchel is filled with cobs of sweet corn and a giant head of cauliflower, the weight of abundance slanting my shoulder downward to the cobblestone street below. Shopping ceases once pockets are emptied of sterling. Mila and I perambulate with Joy down alleyways and past storefronts, and meander into a quiet mews. Through the contemporary wooden door of her home, we wander into a sophisticated Narnia sanctuary, hidden from pedestrian view.

Perched on barstools anchored around a white marble island, we nibble from a charcuterie decorated with jams, pastries, cheeses, and fresh bread. The aroma of fresh squeezed orange juice woos us to sip and savor the refreshing scent. The presentation of food on the island echoes perfectly placed provocative artwork hanging on walls and the monochrome symmetry of pottery containing a harmony of hydrangea plants in the garden. The clean charcoal lines of counters against pristine white cabinets create a pleasing contrast for a bowl of plums blushing pink from yellow. Enchanted by the artistry of an architect and interior designer who live in the home.

Impotent to document the hidden beauty of a friend's house with my camera, words, phrases, and poetry emerge into story playing out in my head. Captivated by color, light, symmetry, and design, my mind pulses with inspired creativity. I can hardly wait to sit down and write words into sentences and paragraphs. The peregrinatio journey cannot be rushed, and contemplating beauty leads me deeper into discovering the attributes of God.

Lost in the detritus of life—deadlines, emails, shopping, carpooling, diapers—we are prone to pass over the inspiration of beauty for the counterfeit of watching beautiful people live from small screens resting in palms and from big screens propped up in living rooms. Rarely do we find other people's stories and plots watched from the couch a satisfaction satiating emptiness. To participate in beauty is to submit to the divine. And to participate in the certainty of God's love is to submit to the process of being made whole. What we long for becomes realized in beauty because creation cannot be duplicated by comparison and the fear of missing out. Outward engagement with beauty leads to fresh perspective internally. I discovered that anew as I converged with a group of fifteen Americans in Italy.

UPON ARRIVAL AT Villa La Foce in Tuscany, I must look like a dumbstruck child wandering through a maze of opulent bedrooms. Decorated with upholstered headboards, painted furniture, gilded armchairs, and brocade couches, the villa translates like an Italian Downton Abbey. Wide-eyed and slack-jawed, I keep thinking, *How did I end up here? How did I get selected to be among these amazing people to experience this beautiful, mystifying place?*

The welcome tour finishes with several of us congregating on the breakfast porch overlooking the Val d'Orcia. Canopied by climbing roses and wisteria vines twisting around columns and hanging from the facade, I point past the dripping fountain swimming with goldfish to a hedge of ancient cypress and declare, "I think I've seen enough for now. I'll save that view of the valley for later." My friends Christie and Kimberly nod and smile in agreement. We're all 4s on the enneagram and need to savor beauty slowly to fully comprehend a wealth of emotions and make meaning of what it is we're thinking.

Once clothes are unpacked into drawers and flowery dresses hang in the wardrobe, I claim a place in the arc of fellow writers standing under an evergreen oak as the sun slowly descends, gilding the landscape. Listening to the smooth, calming voice of Sibylla, our garden tour guide, the disarming tone and cadence of her accent is distractingly reminiscent of Meryl Streep playing the part of Karen in *Out of Africa*. Even the characters surrounding the Renaissance house translate as storylike, beguiling.

Armed with camera, I follow the slanted shadows of new friends down a stone path, past geometrical rooms created with box hedge, stopping at the overlook. Though my eyes are open and heart expectant as I walk, what I am experiencing down the path leading to the overlook isn't visible to anyone but me. The unseen in my soul is seen in the beauty we witness corporately.

For weeks, maybe months, when I close my eyes to pray about the unknowns plaguing my writing life, a scene replays in my mind.

It first emerged while seated in a comfy armchair inside my house. I saw myself walking through a hushed forest of tall pines, a peregrini following Jesus up a flat place on a mountain. The hem of his robe creating a susurration of vagrant leaves, releasing the pleasant ripe scent of dewy petrichor underneath. Beyond a crowd of trunks, the sun drenches a spacious place from pale to verdant, but I have no idea what lies past the forest from our vantage point. *Will there be people waiting for us? A home to visit? A vista of epic proportions to blow my socks off? Where are we going?* Each time I revisit the scene, more questions are added. All I know is that what I'm seeing in my mind's eye translates as preparation for something on the horizon. Like a child trusting in her father's judgment, I anticipate the surprise will be good and worth the climb.

In Tuscany, as I funnel into the crowd collecting at the overlook, internally I am following Jesus through the woods again. The image of the forest flashes unannounced between each step, as if I am being transported while simultaneously present. While Sibylla's mouth is moving, sharing pertinent details about the legacy of the garden created by Antonio and Iris Origo, the faint whisper I'm hearing is not her voice. *We are almost there. This is what I wanted to show you.* "[I] heard the sound of words but saw no form; there was only a voice" (Deuteronomy 4:12).

As the official photographer of the 2018 Tuscany Writers Retreat, I am fully prepared to frame the towering cypress glimpsed from the breakfast patio when we first arrived. Poised behind the lens, I prepare to frame awe depicted on faces. But instead, a wave of God's love drowns all sense of sensibility when I capture with my eyes the beautiful panoramic view before us. Turning away from the scene, I take a second to catch my breath and stop the well of emotions from releasing through tears. From the grandeur of the formal garden to the painted landscape of the Mount Amiata, the view translates as overwhelming, too magnificent a gift to receive.

At the intersection of the past and present—the mingling of our Polaroid history with God's panorama perspective—is the place of unexplainable peace, incomprehensible awe, overwhelming love, and unadulterated beauty. Beauty provides a reorientation toward the hopeful vision God has for us. "God often gives us a hopeful vision of things to come before any of it makes sense," writes Emily P. Freeman after she visited La Foce two years earlier.[3]

WE DESIRE PLACES of milk and honey long before what we desire makes rational sense to us. In Tuscany, it's as if God is pointing his finger: Here is a cypress. Here are quilts made from golden wheat, red poppies, and green olives. Here is a castle on a hill overlooking all that I have made for you. Here is a winery on the flat place of a hill with roots extending six feet below the surface. Here is my blood poured out in a stemmed glass. Sip, savor, swallow my abundance, and allow my love to satiate the unanswered questions of life. Tuscany, I think, is like the Israelites experiencing his powerful presence and backing away from Mount Sinai—overwhelmed by beauty, I feel small and fear being overtaken.

From a vintner in Italy, I learn that every day is written in the grape, and it's possible to discern the taste of wind in wine; that the aroma of an olive is more important than how it tastes, and olive oil scented like fresh grass growing on a sunny day is the best to drizzle on a piece of grilled salmon. Under lapis lazuli sky and floating slabs of white marble clouds, I discover that I am deeply rooted in the United States like grapevines growing for generations in Italy, but the wine of my life is produced in living as a peregrini.

Beholding the beauty of cut flowers and produce at the stalls of a fresh market, beholding the artistry and design of a friend's beautiful house in London, and beholding the tranquil landscapes of Tuscany are a discovery of new details in God's personality, like tassels the Israelites wore back in the day as reminders of His holiness. "Throughout the generations to come you are to make tassels on the corners of your garments, with a blue cord on each tassel. You will have these tassels to look at and so you will remember all the commands of the LORD, that you may obey them and not prostitute yourselves by chasing after the lusts of your own hearts and eyes" (Numbers 15:38–39).

But what does *behold*, that ancient, rarely used word in our vocabulary, mean for us today? In the King James Bible, *behold* is used well over a thousand times, but *behold* is eliminated altogether from Scripture in *The Message*. Today, *behold* has transmuted into an idiom that slips off the tongue when we are surprised by stumbling onto something—*Lo and behold, I finally found the reading glasses I lost perched on top of my head.*

The organic meaning of *behold* is to see, view, face, look out, regard, watch, and consider. In spiritual practices, *behold* is to earnestly contemplate and purposely perceive in order to apprehend the whereabouts of God. When we behold beauty, we are beholding the Beautiful One, and in turn, beholding our lives and the details of our surroundings through the lens of love; discerning the mundane with spiritual eyes. As a child, though unaware at the time, I was beholding the simplicity of beauty in sunlight drawing shadows by his hand on my bedroom wall. Because what we behold in a moment, we remember vividly with the passage of time.

Perhaps *behold* has vanished from our vocabulary for the same reason we can no longer identify with the definition; why we no longer wear tassels on the corners of our clothes. In our hurry-up world, we have severed the blue cord that reminds us to slow down and identify God's palpable presence. We stop only to pay attention to what is displayed on the screens of devices held in our palms; pause only to hear what is playing through earbuds. Ceasing from work only to focus on scrolling to capture what other people are saying on social media. Multitasking only to accomplish what? How do we behold in a fast-paced, harried world? What is captivating your attention from beholding God's whereabouts in your world?

THE MORE WE savor the essence of who God is in Scripture, the more our appetites for his grandeur increases. The more we behold the foreign details of his attributes, the more a longing grows for the majesty of his presence in the mundane. The more we listen and wait, a longing to linger in what we hear deepens. I could tell you about decades of dreams centered around living in London, scheming trips to Italy with H since the dawn of our marriage, but most of all, I want to tell you that the realization of the panorama of those dreams surpass the Polaroids I envisioned.

> The more we *savor* the essence of who God is in Scripture, the more our *appetites* for his grandeur increases.

Eugene Peterson reminds me that, "The lived Christian life always occurs in a place. It is never an abstraction, never generality, never a technique. Place: Shechem, Sinai, Galilee, Bethany, Kalispell. Geography is every bit as essential to the Christian life as theology."[4] And perhaps I can be bold enough to include beauty as essential to our theology too. In the same way God envisioned the beauty of the Temple before Bezalel and Oholiab made his dwelling place a reality, God has a vision for your life and the details are his to unfold into reality. We are exiles searching for true home, and God is creating a sense of permanence through beautiful details in your surroundings.

A hand-painted vase from Montepulciano decorates a corner of my desk and holds dried flowers pulled fresh from the overlook. A round bar of soap from La Foce remains in my carry-on, the scent reminding me that God's presence is near and his love is beautiful. These are my blue tassels carried home from Italy. "Behold, this is our God, we have waited for him, that he might save us. This is the LORD; we have waited for him; let us be glad and rejoice in his salvation" (Isaiah 25:9 ESV).

Practice BEHOLDING BEAUTY FOR THE WILDERNESS OF BEDLAM

How does beauty inform the way you live?

If beauty exists only because God exists, how does that truth change the way you interpret symmetry, harmony, and order in your world?

How might beauty provide the certainty you are searching for amid the unknowns of life?

What scents remind you of hope?

Read Exodus 36. How are the details of the temple important for us today?

How are the details of your life important for inviting peace into disruption?

What kind of beauty is God asking you to create as a sign of his permanence in the uncertainties of life?

Document the simple beauties you experience in your home this week, e.g., shadows forming picture art on the wall.

NINE

Rest When Shadowed by Worry

When the world is a flurry of frenzy, God
shakes our familiarities
like a snow globe
cupped in the hands of a mesmerized child

The cares of life settle
the hush of peace falls
stillness blankets anxiety

Fresh whispers of love

TWO NIGHTS BEFORE Christmas, quiet stillness covers our
row of London terrace houses. From the second floor inside the
house, perched on a stool in front of the dressing table, I look up
and out, past fairy lights hanging from a cardboard star in our
round bedroom window, and locate the moon beaming in a sea
of blackness. Surveying the pavement below, the neighborhood

is reminiscent of Chernobyl, eerily vacant under the harsh yellow glow of a lone streetlamp. The only signs of life ascertained is my tired reflection moving in the glass.

Reaching over collections of perfume bottles, cosmetic brushes, and tubes of lipsticks, I open the metal lid on a glass jar and retrieve a cotton ball when the *ting* of a notification from the phone lying on the nightstand interrupts a familiar bedtime routine. At 10:34 p.m., I read a message from Murielle, sent from Raleigh, North Carolina. For her, it's 5:34 p.m. in the balmy South, where she's returned home after finishing a final holiday shift at Starbucks. Packing a suitcase in preparation for flying to London, her rhythm is halted by a harrowing discovery.

"Hey, Mom. So, I still have to look through some stuff, but my passport wasn't where I thought it was. I was wondering if you, by any chance, saw it when you were here?"

Two months earlier, in mid-October, I was a guest in her apartment between speaking engagements in Austin and Nashville. A detour to Raleigh made presence possible between us after nine months of being separated by an ocean. I nearly missed her entire twenty-first year.

Relishing the opportunity to simply be her mom in the flesh instead of parenting by text, I enjoyed cooking Murielle's favorite meals, tidying up her apartment, and washing laundry. With her permission, I organized spices in the kitchen and household cleaners in the laundry room. She didn't have time to tackle those mundane tasks between two jobs. Mentally retracing the contents of the drawers in her bedroom, I wrote back promptly.

"No, I don't remember seeing it, honey."

"Okay, I figured not. I feel like it is somewhere obvious, and I'm missing it. I'll just look through my apartment," she writes back.

Collapsing on the bed before finishing the process of removing makeup, I stare at the ceiling and retrace mental paper trails, hoping for a new discovery. But the more I strive to find the hidden passport virtually, the more anxiety surfaces in the form of what-ifs. In less than twenty-four hours, our daughter is scheduled to board a transatlantic flight that lands in London on Christmas morning. *What if she misses the flight? What if she can't find her passport? What if she misses our family Christmas holiday altogether?*

Pondering my daughter's simple passport inquiry turns delightful anticipation of a family holiday into a haze of uncertainty. Questions mutate into a cloud of worry prayers, making it impossible to drift off to sleep.

Why? Why, God? Why now? Why must we experience emotional upheaval when we long for peace? Why is our life in London veiled by uncertainty and stress? We long for a celebration of your abundance. We are weary and desire rest, though it seems turmoil is your choice for us instead. Are you paying attention to our prayers? Your silence is deafening, and response, slow as snails. Is your desire for us to simply endure instead of fully live?

Lying in bed with my back toward H, knees curled up to my chest, legs frozen in a fetal position as if holding worry will somehow move God into action on Murielle's behalf. Praying for Murielle to find her passport, *all will be well*, I think, if I just stay here like a warrior holding worry as a shield of protection for a little while. A few minutes later, legs unfurl in the sudden stream of texts.

Fairy lights in the window, set by a timer, click off at 11:15 p.m., but my mind still blazes with what-ifs. Though an ocean separates us, together Murielle and I virtually uncover all the possible places a passport might be concealed—the crowded drawers of her desk, the glove box in the car, suitcase pockets, the bottom of her backpack, and the entrails of every purse. She fastidiously scours every crease, crevice, and crack, double-checking until all the obvious places are exhausted.

Uncertainty quickly reorients me back to an unstable childhood and the false belief that worry is my work for claiming peace. Maybe you have experienced that too? Finding peace in the middle minutes of the unknown can be challenging when we focus on the *whys* and *what-ifs*. But when we focus on the Father heart of God, worry mutates into peace.

At midnight in London, my conversation with her halts and body shifts. Tucking socked feet under a puffy duvet, I recite the Lord's Prayer. *Our Father who art in heaven, hallowed be thy name* . . . until the armor of worry releases, and I drift off to sleep.

At 5 a.m. on Christmas Eve in London, I awaken to darkness, roll over, and find H's eyes open. Holding his mobile phone like a Bible over his chest, he's praying and waiting for a happy ending. But a new notification from Murielle causes a second swell of panic.

Her passport was left in a friend's car after a summer road trip to our family cottage in Canada, several months earlier. The problem is that car is not in North Carolina, but in Alabama, where her friend is visiting relatives.

The passport wasn't lost in the underbelly of her bedroom, it was safely tucked away with an oil change record, traveling hundreds of miles away from where she needed it to gain entrance into England.

Assessing potential options for expediting a passport overnight, we quickly come to unified conclusion: There isn't a single scenario that allows those vital documents to reach Raleigh before her flight leaves for London. H and I lie still in bed, hold hands, and independently envision our first Christmas without our firstborn. I long to cry, but I am stubborn.

An hour later, a new message arrives detailing a bold plan she has hatched to liaise with her friend in Greenville, South Carolina, the halfway point for each of them. Driving eight hours through the middle of the night on no sleep? I wonder if I am still dreaming.

Worry pushes my feet from under the warm duvet to pacing the kitchen, clicking the kettle on, unloading the dishwasher, filling drawers with clean towels, typing last-minute grocery lists, and wrapping stocking stuffers in green and red tissue paper. "It says somewhere that God's grace comes and goes, with no fault of ours, and when we do not have it, we wait patiently, and it returns. I do think manual labor of one kind or another is of help and when I get in states which last, I get to housecleaning," writes Dorothy Day, and I couldn't agree more.[1]

A quotidian housecleaning rhythm helps push the implications of two people driving separately through the night on no sleep to the fringes of the false narratives I'm creating with my imagination. Because on top of everything, Murielle's mobile phone has gone black. For almost a week, she's been messaging with us from her laptop during the hours she isn't at work. But now, communication with us, or anyone for that matter, isn't possible on the long commute. That middle-of-the-night Vox we missed from her when we first landed in London is still fresh in the forefront of thoughts. The silence surrounding our uncertainty is deafening, so we do the only thing left in our power: We pray like it's our job, intercede like our prayers are toothpicks holding their eyelids open. Like Moses stretching his arms over the Red Sea, we pray for the Lord to open a path that allows for her to reach us in time for Christmas. And we invite friends to hold our arms up in prayer too.

ENTER AN UNWANTED situation, and all your familiar coping mechanisms go dark, like a lifeline connected to the outer world suddenly cut off. All the things you used as ways to assign value and worth to your life become idols replacing God in their absence. The realization is both a grief and a freedom; an opening of vulnerability that allows for an intersection of the immutability of God with the mundane.

An Advent reading on December 23 seems providential and poignant now as I reread it under the lens of this new situation. Ann Voskamp writes, "We are not spared of all trials, but we are always spared of the trials that have no gifts. God always gives God. We can always have as much of God as we want. What is stretching Mary's skin is God and what is always stretching us is God."[2]

The way of the peregrini is stretching and costly. "It means becoming a stranger and an exile to all that is familiar, safe," Esther de Waal tells us. "But the peregrini found an example in Christ who willingly came down from heaven and so they could look towards him and see that voluntary exile is laudable since it is in the imitation of Christ himself. It is an exile that demands the stripping of family and possessions, the rooting out from heart and mind of all one's own aims and desires."[3] While Murielle wanders outwardly in search of a missing passport, I wander inwardly as a peregrini by telling myself the truth about who God is despite the shadow of uncertainty over our family Christmas.

At times God reveals himself openly, and other times he is an apparition, dwelling mysteriously in the darkness. And "the people remained at a distance, while Moses approached the thick darkness where God was" (Exodus 20:21). For six days, the glory of God was manifest as a thick cloud covering Mount Sinai, but it wasn't until the seventh day, the day of rest, that the Lord called to Moses from within the cloud. It is when we are at rest that we hear the voice of God echoing over our worry.

> It is when we are at *rest* that we hear the voice of God *echoing* over our worry.

Though it feels as if my faith is like a helium balloon avoiding a pinprick, in rest, I meditate on a litany of coaching questions that cause fear to float away and the truth to rise again.

If this trial is a gift, then what might God have in mind for us?

Is there any circumstance where God is not present?

If he loves my daughter more than I do, what situation is beyond his care for her?

Where am I lacking trust? And what exactly am I trusting in?

Clarity and peace return as I cling to a string of certainties inherent in God's attributes. If he is working all things together for our good, this scenario isn't an exception. He is not a 50 percent Father, he is 100 percent all-in. He is cheering us on and choosing to be with us; with us in loss and in what is found; with us in what we long for but have yet to fully grasp.

While Moses was insulated by the cloud of God's glory, "to the Israelites the glory of the LORD looked like a consuming fire on top of the mountain" (Exodus 24:17). For forty days and nights, while Moses had a mountaintop experience, chiseling notes into stone with his finger—*make, build, command, serve, tell, bring, offer, take, rest*—final instructions before Moses traipsed back down the mountain were this: "Say to the Israelites, 'You must observe my Sabbaths. This will be a sign between me and you for generations to come, so you may know that I am the LORD, who makes you holy'" (Exodus 31:13). But the Israelites weren't at rest; they became restless in the waiting and decided to help God out just a little bit by making a golden calf.

We fear that life won't turn out the way we hope. Worry ensues because we want to control problems. Therefore, this false narrative becomes a familiar mantra: *If I can control my problems, then I can solve them, avoiding disappointment and hardship.* Creating golden calves is the greatest compromise the enemy hopes we'll accept. Today our golden calves look like climbing into debt for wants over needs, controlling kids' college entrance exams, manipulating conversations toward preferred outcomes, opening doors based on popularism rather than wisdom, jumping into "get rich quick" schemes, volunteering from fear rather than passion, reacting rather than waiting on love to respond.

"Excessive worry activates the amygdala housed in the limbic system of the brain, while short circuiting our prefrontal cortex. The limbic system is the 'emotional center' of our brain that controls 'fight or flight.' Fight or flight is a primitive mechanism going back to the cavemen that keeps us safe from danger. When a person excessively worries, this mechanism becomes overactive, releasing excessive amounts of adrenaline, causing us to see dangers that are not really there or to overestimate danger.

Thus, excessive worrying hijacks the amygdala housed in the limbic system and shuts off, or derails, the prefrontal lobe of the brain, which regulates rational thinking. Thus, you become 'emotionally activated' versus calm and rational in your thinking. This strong emotional charge makes it hard, if not impossible, to find solutions to life challenges."[4]

I come from a long line of worriers who are emotionally activated versus calm and rational. The branches of my genealogy hang with images of worst-case scenarios; our DNA infused by certitude as the idol we pick from the tree when ravenous for control about future outcomes. But some of us have been grafted into the truth by believing that "whoever dwells in the shelter of the Most High will rest in the shadow of the Almighty." Worry keeps me stuck in the same place, but staying tucked under the armpit of the Most High means moving forward in faith. "He is my refuge and my fortress, my God, in whom I trust" (Psalm 91:1–2). When Moses wrote Psalm 91, he knew from experience that God offers us more than situational safety and security; he offers the certainty of his sovereignty sheltering us. "He will cover you with his pinions, and under his wings you will find refuge; his faithfulness is a shield and buckler" (Psalm 91:4 ESV).

The pinion is the outer part of a bird's wing including the flight feathers, the terminal section of a bird's wing. Therefore, the pinion is the most vulnerable part of a bird's anatomy. Without those wings, they cannot fly. Psalm 91 is a foreshadowing of Jesus giving his life for us. "Like an eagle that stirs up its nest and hovers over its young, that spreads its wings to catch them and carries them aloft" (Deuteronomy 32:11), God not only provides safety but bears the weight of rescuing us.

Saturating the mind with truth about God's character and nature means revelatory peace overshadows fear. Worry transmutes into reassurances when the mind is focused on his attributes.

You will not fear the terror of night, nor the arrow that flies by day, nor the pestilence that stalks in the darkness, nor the plague that destroys at midday. A thousand may fall at your side, ten thousand at your right hand, but it will not come near you.

Psalm 91:5–7

We can't get to intimacy outside of vulnerability. And if uncertainty is a vulnerability, is it also an opportunity for deepening relationship with him? *Why would God do that for me?* might be the most mysterious question we can never fully solve outside of faith.

Christmas is about Jesus coming into the world, doing whatever it takes to be with us. Is it possible that a displaced passport is a subversive act of love like no room at the inn on the day of Christ's birth? Could wandering to find what is missing cause us to find him in the most unexpected places? What revelation might come in the search for certainty? What truth might we discover in the disruptions of life? Could he be waiting for us to acknowledge his presence like the wise men wandering toward a chiaroscuro God? What hope might God illuminate in the shadow of what we know but cannot see clearly?

> If uncertainty is a *vulnerability*, is it also an opportunity for *deepening* relationship with God?

Chiaroscuro is an oxymoron, a mid-seventeenth-century word from *chiaro* meaning clear, bright (from Latin *clarus*) and *oscuro* meaning dark, obscure (from Latin *obscurus*), Italian for light and shadow. Rooted in classic techniques used in the works of artists like Rembrandt, da Vinci, and Caravaggio, *chiaroscuro* refers to the use of light and shadow to create the illusion of light from a specific source shining on the figures and objects in the painting. Originating from the Renaissance period and often associated with painting or drawing, it has evolved into use among photographers to define strong and bold contrasts between light and dark areas in a photograph, especially portraits and still life in black-and-white photos. Adding depth and mysterious atmosphere, chiaroscuro creates impact and contrast between highlights and shadows.

A peregrini can live in harmony with a chiaroscuro God, live in the tension of light and shadow when the world uses black and white as a measuring stick for peace, purpose, and potential. Because a peregrini has no specific end goal in mind—not a place to arrive, not a number to reach, not a plan to achieve or a mission fulfilled—just an inner prompting to go, declaring *pro amore Christi*, or for the love of Christ, because he loved you first. The peregrinatio journey is not made up of exiles but guests of the world. Because where can you wander that God cannot be found with you?

AT MURIELLE'S AGE, my faith was stretched when I too embarked upon driving through the night without a cell phone, following the glare of red taillights on a car driven by college friends Andra and Bill, leading the way from Oklahoma to Arizona. But unlike my daughter, the journey wasn't about visiting relatives but beginning a new chapter of my life. Relatively sure the trek was about living in Phoenix permanently though my Midwestern feet had never set foot in the desert. It wasn't a passport I was missing but all the concrete assurances that landing in Arizona would prove sustainable. Like the wise men navigating the journey toward the Christ child by the brightness of a star rather than a map or compass, I was moving forward without a job, place to live, savings account, or connections for obtaining all those things in a new city. Hope was my pathway to trust. At twenty-one, graduating from university during an economic downturn, my peregrinatio journey to Arizona began by giving God an ultimatum the night before loading my Honda CRX with all my worldly possessions. *I'm not getting up from this couch until you show me if this is right. It's up to you to keep me from making the worst decision of my life.* Wise or foolish, basically, I was being true to my three-year-old self again.

The next morning, I awaken in the guest bedroom of my mother's house to a chiaroscuro landscape when a winter storm hits Tulsa, the worst weather in decades. Sunshine creates charcoal shadows on a white canvas, and vacant streets are museums of light and iridescence. Towering maple trees transform into giant glass figurines. But branches begin breaking from bearing too much weight, the haunting sound cracking open the eerie stillness as ice shatters like a million crystal vases thrown from the top of a skyscraper. Thousands are without power, but my tank is full of gas and my trunk is stuffed with idealism. Wheels crunch over ice as I slowly pull away from my mother's gingerbread house in the Cherry Street district of Tulsa.

Arriving in the painted mountains of Arizona by day's end, we pause overnight, sleeping in the house of Bill's parents in Flagstaff. And one simple question asked during the one and only short conversation I ever had with the Miller family, leads to making one of the biggest decisions that changes the trajectory of my life. Can you recommend a church in Phoenix?

Valley Cathedral is their answer. Worshiping on the first Sunday after arriving safely in Phoenix, I make Valley Cathedral my church home when the theme of the sermon is on the pastor's peregrinatio faith journey from his home in the South to Phoenix, Arizona. A coincidence or God-incidence?

AFTER A FEW weeks with little success at securing a job, money is running low and I issue another ultimatum, talking to God in the bathroom mirror. *If I don't get a job soon, I'll have no other choice but to turn back. If you want me to stay in Phoenix, then show me with a job offer by the end of the week.* And he answers with a position behind a makeup counter at a department store. Staying in Phoenix was God's providence as I met and married

HG Miller at Valley Cathedral and gave birth to our two children years later. My friend Andra and I both end up taking the last name of Miller through marriage, completely random and unrelated.

If you think giving God an ultimatum is wrong, Moses illustrates something different. He tells God, "If your Presence does not go with us, do not send us up from here. How will anyone know that you are pleased with me and with your people unless you go with us? What else will distinguish me and your people from all the other people on the face of the earth?" And God answers, "I will do the very thing you have asked, because I am pleased with you and I know you by name" (Exodus 33:1–17).

An ultimatum isn't a tactic of control and manipulation but a heartfelt, honest prayer about the realities we're facing. It's the opposite of control; it's a prayer of surrender to the omniscience of God. An ultimatum in this context communicates, *I know very little, but you are all-knowing, and I am desperate for your favor.*

AS I RELEASE the plans I once envisioned for a family Christmas through the practice of resting my mind with the truth about God's character and attributes, the contrast of false narratives created by worry become evident. The clock is no longer a bully but a gift. Rational thought replaces my propensity toward the fight instinct. When H gallops down the stairs, updating us with news received by text, that Murielle has reached Greenville safely, revelation comes in the word *safe*. When **S**urrendered to the **A**lmighty **F**or **E**ternal perspective rather than surrendered to self to achieve temporal comfort, an uncharacteristically calm center results. Though time ticks toward Murielle's imminent departure at the airport, my soul is stilled in the knowledge that we are fully known and deeply loved. I see with new eyes, like the people of Israel who saw the mighty power of the Lord unleashed on the banks of the Red Sea. The frames in my story are filled with awe as I focus on the certainty of God's faithfulness. I can rest in the possibility of a different outcome.

As dusk descends on Christmas Eve, fairy lights click on, creating shadows on the ceiling, warming up an otherwise dark and drafty house. Wrapped gifts are stacked underneath the Christmas tree and food is prepped for a traditional celebratory dinner. Everything is ready for receiving the miracle of Christ's presence. I crawl under the duvet, lie on my side, and rest a cheek on the fluffed pillow. A tear releases, gently slopes downward, drops and dissolves into cotton sheets. When we awaken on Christmas morning, there are no new notifications from Murielle on our phones.

"We are a generation of tired people, longing to see evidence that what we wait for in secret is worth it. We believe and want help in our unbelief. Our souls make quiet work of always scanning for truth. When we find it, the tears spill over and take us by surprise," writes Emily P. Freeman.[5] And I am surprised by the visceral miracle of peace ascertained, overshadowing worry caused by uncertainty over the past twenty-four hours. Within the mystery, a miracle is waiting to be birthed. Wandering is where the journey toward promise begins.

"HOW ARE THEY?" I ask H when he appears in the doorway, chewing.

Testing the warm nut ball cookies cooling on metal sheets in the kitchen, traces of powdered sugar dust his chin when he reports, after swallowing, "They're good, different texture and a bit more buttery, but good."

"I think they taste good," Murielle assesses, licking powdered sugar off her fingers.

Good, but not quite the same is the mantra echoed among the four of us as we celebrate Christmas in a different country.

Green food coloring for marshmallow wreath cookies is less green and more like cloudy puddle water. Sausage balls are made with the help of a recipe for Jimmy Dean culled from the internet, made with Red Leicester cheese rather than Colby. The kids summarize, "Good, but not quite the same" while eating breakfast on Christmas morning and dinner, later that evening. And could it be that celebrating in the shadow of past experience is exactly what God intended for us, in order that the Light of his presence might illuminate misplaced hope. Hope placed in things we can control when his uncontrollable presence overshadows our limited expectations. Because we do not have a continuing city and the "'insider world' is not our home. We have our eyes peeled for the City about to come" (Hebrews 13:14 *The Message*). What disorientation do we face that God is not capable of reorienting toward his promises? What shadow do we encounter that Light cannot illuminate with wonder?

> Tattered seraphim flash their diminishing
> edges, like the chiaroscuro God who,
> if we believe Michelangelo, touched
> Adam into being with one finger,
> whose footprints crease the blackness
> of Gennesaret, whose wing feathers brush
> our vaulted heaven, purple with storm,
> whose moon is smudged—a round, glass window,
> an eye moving between clouds.
>
> An excerpt from Luci Shaw's poem,
> *St. Frideswide's Chapel*[6]

Practice Rhythms of Rest
for the Wilderness of Worry

Cease from finding solutions and projecting outcomes. Pause in silence and visualize God as refuge, fortress, shield, and buckler. How does that exercise change the narrative you are currently telling yourself?

What expectations are you holding that God is asking you to release into his care?

How might your need for certainty be an idol replacing God in your situation?

Write down the visceral responses you are experiencing due to uncertainty. Release each one of them back to him. What is God not capable of handling on your behalf?

Meditate on Psalm 91 line by line. Rehearse the truth of God's character back to him through adoration, e.g., verse 1: "Those who live in the shelter of the Most High will find rest in the shadow of the Almighty." *Lord, I adore you for sheltering me. Thank you that your presence shadows me wherever I go.* How do his attributes inform your circumstances?

If God is working all things together for your good, how might your untimely uncertainty be God's good timing for you?

Are you willing to risk waiting, or will your need for certainty keep you from trusting in the mystery?

TEN

Named and Known

What's in a name
that makes you listen or turn away?

Names assign hope
to what is rudderless, adrift, tangled.

Hope is hearing your name
spoken as a whisper.

Your name is a revelation
Keeping you from falling into familiarity.

You are not alone in the unknown.
You are known.

GROWING UP, FEAR of the dark moves me from sleeping alone in a twin bed to switching places with Grandpa on weekends; curling up beside Grandma before the lamps switch off at night. As morning dawns, I awaken to the sound of the garage door closing. Grandma has quietly slipped out of bed to attend early morning mass while Grandpa is puttering around the house. Sleepy eyes linger over the black and white portraits of each set of great-grandparents, framed side by side on the wall in the corner of their bedroom. Repeatedly on weekends, they both independently point to Grandma's mother in one of the photos and describe a similar sentiment that sounds something like this: "We wish you could've known your Great-Grandmother Smith; she was such a special person."

What was so different about her? What was it about her character that provokes remarks apart from the others captured in the old photographs? Every weekend, I stare at the portraits, memorizing smartly dressed people smiling for the photographer, attempting to find clues to the mystery, that special something that sets Harriet Smith apart. Because what I hear behind their remarks about my great-grandmother is this: *You remind us of her.*

Decades later, the rumble of tires on pavement awakens me from a sound sleep in London, and those mysterious unknowns about my great-grandmother bubble to the surface of first thoughts. I hadn't thought about her in years. Composing a quick email to Dad, I ask him to fill in the unknown-to-me details of the mysterious great-grandmother that still haunt me.

The following day, I make note in my journal about awakening from a dream and replaying the hilarity out loud to H: Uncharacteristically, I have chosen prostitution as a vocation for making money, but conviction won't allow me to go through with it. We laugh in tandem.

But that bizarre, out-of-the-blue dream mutates into something more meaningful when a few hours later, I receive an email from Dad in response to my inquisitiveness. It turns out that the monochrome photo I was using for clues about my history was impotent to reveal her colorful past. Unsubstantiated rumors that Great-Grandma was a prostitute before marrying Howard Smith.

The serendipity of that crazy dream with the timing of my curiosity about a great-grandmother I hadn't thought about in years suddenly seem more like meaningful clues leading to something important rather than random coincidence. Why the repetition of *prostitution* when I rarely use that word in my vocabulary? It isn't as much about the act of prostitution—after all, Jesus is a direct descendant of Rahab, a prostitute—but about what is being conveyed in the repetition. What might God be trying to convey beyond the obvious? Why is such an evocative word being highlighted right now? Repetition is often God's modus operandi for garnering our attention; for discovery, assigning deeper meaning, and clarifying purpose. He succeeded in capturing my full attention with the sacred echo.

As I read the details of Great-Grandma's history, remembered with fondness and respect by my father, I learn that Harriet was born a German immigrant, grew up poor and uneducated, and married Howard Smith on the rebound when his relationship with a socialite in St. Louis fell apart. "She took people as she found them without placing stipulations on relationships," Dad writes.

Converting to Catholicism after marriage, she is described as devout, serious about faith. Was that what my grandparents were referring to when they thought about her attributes? Howard Smith passes away first and Dad fills in as taxi driver, picking up his grandmother for routine Sunday dinners, walking down flights of stairs as she holds on to his arm for balance. She wears straight skirts, sweaters, and heels into her eighties. Dad recalls stopping mid-step when a brand-new red Corvette whizzes past. Turning to make eye contact, she admits, "I would own that car if I could drive."

She is the responsible adult who stays home with the kids while the parents travel, extending permission for parties while trusted to keep quiet about the ruse. A woman who arises from deep sleep to listen rather than advise the grief of young love, into the wee hours of night when Dad suffers a breakup with a girlfriend. The woman with whom I never have the pleasure of making eye contact or discerning the cadence of her voice feels kindred the more I learn about her. She relishes reading books, enjoys the art of conversation and storytelling. Characterized by curiosity and exploration, she enjoys travel to new places, cooking for family, creating traditions, enjoying the arts and new culture, and walking rather than driving from place to place. While I have yet to drive in London, I learn that Great-Grandma Smith never owned a car or driver's license while living in St. Louis.

It was as if my dad's memory confirmed the inklings I had as a child. *Yes, her DNA is living on in you.* But what does all this mean? How is this information pertinent for me now? What is God attempting to show me about my family of origin? As I pray, wait, and listen, a warning surfaces providing new definition.

Don't prostitute your gifts by discounting the value of what they bring into the world. You prostitute yourself with resignation—"this is just the way life is," rather than waiting on me with this glorification—"this is how God intends for me to trust him." I live within the art that is your life, and when you acquiesce, you are prostituting my power planned to move in people's hearts through your life.

Specifically, I prostituted the gift of writing by agreeing to author a book for a sum of money that was laughably undervalued for the time investment. Wooed by a British editor who charmed me with an invitation to meet shortly after landing in England, I was traipsed around the publishing house and inserted into lunch among executives. And completely blindsided by an offer to publish anything I wanted because my writing was impressive to him. Twenty minutes of brainstorming led to a signed contract. No book proposal or platform statics required. The publishing house declared bankruptcy the week I turned in the completed manuscript.

You prostituted yourself by accepting less than what you know my influence is worth. And I am going to redeem what I have given you in that book for my glory. Your righteous indignation about being devalued monetarily is how I feel when my children disregard my power, presence, and purpose in their uncertainty.

We prostitute relationship by using God for our self-interests, devaluing intimacy and holiness inherent in his Fatherhood. God redeemed my grandmother's surreptitious past with love, and he was true to his promise of redemption in the book I wrote but never published. The content was turned into a podcast for my patrons who tell me they glean healing and encouragement from listening. He will do the same for those who follow his commandments and trust that his precepts are good.

> We prostitute *relationship* by using God for our self-interests, devaluing *intimacy* and *holiness* inherent in his Fatherhood.

"God's promises always intersect with places," writes Christie Purifoy. "To remember is to return. To return is to remember. Rootlessness is a kind of forgetting. And home is the dwelling place of memory."[1]

Perhaps it was rootlessness that led to the forgetfulness of Miriam and Aaron as they began complaining, judging Moses based on whom he married—a dark-skinned Cushite woman. Perhaps as unlikely a match as the perfect union between my great-grandparents. The truth behind the disgruntlement is an accusation about Moses being prideful, going about as if he is the only one the Lord speaks through. "What is so special about Moses?" was what, in essence, they were communicating through self-interest. And the Lord heard them. He gathered the three siblings together at the Tent of Meeting like I imagine my H gathering our kids on the front stoop for discipline. If Miriam and Aaron expected to be vindicated by God's agreement with their judgment about Moses, I imagine their cheeks growing pink and hot and shoulders slumping downward, as God explains why Moses is, indeed, special to him.

When there is a prophet among you, I, the Lord, reveal myself to them in visions, I speak to them in dreams. But this is not true of my servant Moses; he is faithful in all my house. With him I speak face to face, clearly and not in riddles; he sees the form of the LORD. Why then were you not afraid to speak against my servant Moses?

Numbers 12:6–8

We are introduced to Miriam as Moses' older sister when she is about six years old. The courageous young girl who follows her baby brother drifting in a basket boat and wisely suggests to Pharaoh's daughter that she find a nurse (her mother). Miriam has the kind of grit I imagine Great-Grandmother Smith beholding. But we don't hear about Miriam for eighty years, until she joins her brothers as a prophetic leader on the pilgrimage to free the Israelites from captivity in Egypt. Devotion to the brother she saved from certain death turns into complaint from self-interest, clouding wise judgment and provoking God's anger.

But his compassion never runs out.

The LORD [Yahweh], the LORD [Yahweh], the compassionate and gracious God, slow to anger, abounding in love and faithfulness, maintaining love to thousands, and forgiving wickedness, rebellion and sin. Yet he does not leave the guilty unpunished; he punishes the children and their children for the sin of the parents to the third and fourth generation.

Exodus 34:6–7

God has a name. It's Yahweh, meaning *He is.* But Exodus tells us that his name is also *Jealous . . .* "Do not worship any other god, for the LORD, whose name is Jealous, is a jealous God" (Exodus 34:14). He is jealous for his name, which ultimately means Yahweh is jealous for his reputation. John Mark Comer writes, "Because Yahweh is locked in relationship with us, there is a symbiotic relationship between Yahweh's *name*— his reputation—and how we, the people of God, *live.* Because Yahweh's name is also *our* name."[2]

As sons and daughters of God, we carry his name as our own. And so, we carry the family name and reputation of the King of kings wherever we go. And he warns us not to prostitute the reputation of the family name by living contrary to his character and attributes.

> Be careful not to make a treaty with those who live in the land; for when they prostitute themselves to their gods and sacrifice to them, they will invite you and you will eat their sacrifices. And when you choose some of their daughters as wives for your sons and those daughters prostitute themselves to their gods, they will lead your sons to do the same.
>
> Exodus 34:15-16

The hidden family secret about Great-Grandma Smith veers into potential truth when I learn she passes away in her eighties, at a sanitarium my father describes as something out of a horror movie, due to complications from syphilis. "I went to see her a couple of times but just could not go back again because it was so spooky," he writes.

But the way she died isn't how people remember her. It wasn't prostitution that led my grandparents pointing to the framed black-and-white portrait, still lingering in grief over her absence. I like to think that Great-Grandma lived true to the reputation of Yahweh in the minds of those who knew her—compassionate, slow to anger, abounding in love and faithfulness. Perhaps punished for the consequences of sin at the end of her days like Miriam who turned leprous, white as snow for seven days, inward darkness reflected on the outside of her body. Leprosy is bodily decay considered to be a "walking death." And during times of uncertainty, God is faithful to reveal what is causing our soul to decay, bringing to light what might become the death of us if allowed to fester in the darkness.

As a child, I was known as Shelly Reeves, inheriting the name and legacy of my father. And as my spiritual knowledge grew at Faith Assembly of God, I identified more with Yahweh than his lofty title as Lord. From knowing about God to owning the family name as His daughter. I wasn't just a teenager tagging along wherever my mother chose to make home, but carrying the family name of Yahweh to school, Girl Scouts, band practice, cheerleader tryouts, and on the several-mile daily journey walking home from school.

When I married H, I inherited the Miller family name and the legacy of godly reputation from both sides of his family. Yahweh distinguishes us as Christians, a name setting us apart as different. And the Lord said (to Moses), "I will do the very thing you have asked because I am pleased with you and I know you by name" (Exodus 33:17). He knows you by name and you carry the family name with you too. When you cycle at the gym, commute to the office, stand in front of kids at a sleepover; when you are placing items from your cart onto the conveyor belt at the grocery store, your true name isn't embossed on your debit card but living within you. And Yahweh embodied my frame in a flannel nightgown as a teenager, when an intruder entered our home hours before sunrise.

JINGLE OF THE front door handle on the house with slanted floors awakens me from a sound sleep. Lying in bed attempting to find clarity in my whereabouts, I assess that Mom is struggling to hold the house key steady enough to insert it into the lock and open the door. After several failed attempts, I slip out of bed and pull the door open from the inside. And find a red-faced man standing next to her wearing overalls, one strap hanging loose over a large beer belly. Stepping inside, Mom bumps into walls, leans shoulders on doorjambs for stability, and he follows her toward the bedroom, giggling. And that's when Yahweh inflates inside of me and I hold on to the heft of his authority.

"You'll have to go home now," I tell the stranger firmly, crossing my arms and blocking the doorway.

"She invited me here," he retorts, towering above me, leaving a halo of alcohol breath between us.

"I think she's not in a place to make that kind of decision; you'll have to go home now," I repeat, pointing toward the front door, insisting with arched eyebrows and puckered lips.

In the time it takes for that short exchange between us, my mother falls asleep. The stranger in our house relents, walking toward the front door, muttering under his breath about having to "walk a long distance because she drove me here."

I lock the front door, turn out the lights, pull the door closed to my mother's bedroom, crawl back underneath warm blankets, and pray myself back to sleep, thanking God. "On the day I called, you answered me; my strength of soul you increased" (Psalm 138:3 ESV). In a few hours, an alarm clock will sound, and I'll reenter the alternate universe among peers sitting in classrooms of high school, feeling like a different person. Brave and confident.

When we are vulnerable, we need gritty people who will stand as practical and spiritual gatekeepers like the Sons of Korah. Our chief concern must be the temple of the heart, being gatekeepers on what we allow to come in and out of our inner world. We need to be people of certainty for others in the trenches too. People who see what others cannot see when judgment is clouded by self-interest and unwanted circumstances. What you allow to come in and out of your mind can cultivate closeness with God or alienate him from your life.

When the cloud lifted, there stood Miriam unaware that she was leprous, like snow. It was her brother Aaron who first saw what she was blind to see on her own. Aaron said to Moses, "Please, my lord, I ask you not to hold against us the sin we have so foolishly committed." And Moses cried out to the Lord, echoing the prayer of my heart for my mother, "Please, God, heal her!" (Numbers 12:11, 13).

We need to be
people of *certainty*
for others
in the *trenches* too.

The God who is slow to anger does gets mad. But as we discover through the Exodus story, he relents. He changes his mind. The word *relent* is *naham* in Hebrew, translated as Yahweh *changed his mind*, or even *repented*. "The word *naham* carries this idea of regret or remorse over a decision. The idea isn't that God was off base, at all; it's that God was moved emotionally; he regretted his decision to judge Israel so harshly, and so he changed his approach."[3]

We have a Father who feels as well as knows. Relents not because he is weak, changeable, insecure, or indecisive but because he understands our humanity and responds as a friend to our circumstances. Emotions and intellect are not mutually exclusive, nor are they always accurate predictors when making judgments. To be in Christ is not to crack the code of having all the right answers or to be led by how we feel, but to be gritty. Choose courage and enter honest conversation with the Creator. He is relational, not a machine providing ticker tapes of right answers or feelings that overshadow rational thought. When you are unrelenting in your requests, God relents.

Research reveals that those who experience a wide range of emotions are happier and healthier than those who limit their feelings.[4] In photography, the tonal range in black-and-whites is one of the most important aspects of aesthetically pleasing images. Range is the degree of brightness and darkness in what you capture, as well as feel. The greater the tonal range, meaning the more dark and light areas there are, the more impressive the image. We need both the light and dark to understand the range of God's great love for us. Without the dark being exposed by the Light, we cannot fathom the depth and breadth of his character and attributes. We cannot comprehend the Light without the risk of exposing the darkness.

The spiritual practice of adoration promotes deliverance from self-interest, ushering us into a mind-set and emotion that leads to being characterized as God-interested. Here is the paradox: As we name God, we declare the range of God's character and nature, and that leads to the discovery of what is black and white about our faith.

Think of Miriam's prayer of adoration when delivered from the Egyptians as a black-and-white portrait hanging on the wall of your home, giving clues to future generations about how to leave a legacy of grit and perseverance. "The LORD is my strength and my defense; he has become my salvation. He is my God, and I will praise him, my father's God, and I will exalt him. The LORD [Yahweh] is a warrior; the LORD [Yahweh] is his name" (Exodus 15:2–3). His *name*, not only a title.

Miriam's song of deliverance is a prayer of response in the conversation with God that began on the Exodus road. And aren't we all exiles walking home, looking for hints about where to turn, which way to go, which path to choose next? We practice adoration, not in hope that it changes God but because adoration changes us into people of hope. We become what we worship. We become that in which we put our trust. Adoration makes us more like Jesus and clarifies what and who are we worshiping. Whom do you adore? Whom do you want to be like?

I want to be like those gritty heroes of the faith who paved the way for us, gritty people like Miriam, Moses, and my great-grandma Smith who overcame obstacles common to all of us yet persevered in trust amid uncertainty. Grit means courage and resolve; strength of character. And it is possible to summon courage and resolve to keep the faith despite life's missteps and disappointments.

Psychologist Angela Lee Duckworth defines *grit* as "the ability to persevere in pursuing a future goal over a long period of time and not giving up. . . . It is having stamina. It's sticking with your future, day-in, day-out, not just for the week, not just for the month, but for years and working really hard to make that future a reality. Grit is living life like it's a marathon, not a sprint."[5] Like Moses sacrificing quiet comfort to lead whining Israelites through the desert for forty years, displaying grit when it wasn't popular or comfortable to do so.

When Miriam's leprosy heals, Moses appoints twelve leaders to scout out the land of Canaan with specific instructions, even though God had already declared the land as *flowing with milk and honey*. In the process of appointments, he changes the name of Hoshea to Joshua. From *I am salvation* to *God is my salvation*. And that slight nuance is a metaphor for what happens when we shift from being led by self-interest versus the interests of God. Forty days later, after the Twelve return from exploration, fear causes the men to give false reports. "We went into the land to which you sent us, and it does flow with milk and honey! Here is its fruit. But the people who live there are powerful, and the cities are fortified and very large" (Numbers 13:27–28).

Only two, Joshua and Caleb, return with the heart of a peregrini, making the switch from cynicism—*let me decide if this is really as good as you say it is*—to the certainty of God's reputation—*I believe what you say, your track record is good despite potential uncertainties*. "Then Caleb silenced the people before Moses and said, 'We should go up and take possession of the land, for we can certainly do it'" (Numbers 13:30).

Unfortunately, the Israelites chose to believe in numbers of voices rather than the two small voices of gritty truth. They wept, grumbled, waxed nostalgic, and wished for death, all based on false narratives created from the fear of ten men. And like a parent listening to a child weep and wail for hours, God had enough and threatened to revoke the milk and honey and send them to their eternal bedrooms. But Moses intervened in compassion, defending his people by debate. Pleading their case led to winning *naham*. God relented by forgiving them. But their grumbling wasn't forgiven without consequences. The ten who chimed in on the false reports were struck down by a plague while Joshua and Caleb remained standing, healthy.

What false narrative have you chosen by listening to popular perspective rather than perspective from listening to the still, small voice? What outcomes are you projecting based on fear of giants rather than the certainty of God's presence in the room?

The outcome of inquisitiveness about my ancestors continues with the discovery that a branch of my tree begins with a name rooted in England. H and I decide to scout out the land, making a trip to Ravenglass in the north of England, to investigate if what we were learning is really true. Is it true that the places we long to make home, the ways in which we desire to live, the passions and pursuits we dream about, and the ways we bring ourselves into the world are not learned, but formed from the very beginning and crying to come out?

"IF I'M BORING you, just flake off," Patrick says to me and the crowd following closely behind him. We're meandering along a grassy terrace for a garden tour in the Lakes District of Cumbria in North England. His blunt honesty provokes giggles and eye contact between strangers who have landed at Muncaster Castle from places around the world. Not a single person turns around and walks away from the ninety-year-old eccentric man wearing a handmade scarf tied around his neck, cane in hand. Patrick changed his name to Pennington when he married his now-deceased wife, moved into the castle, and gave up a lucrative career to cultivate muniments of beauty for others to enjoy. The Pennington name is what brought us hundreds of miles from London, visiting the area.

Trudging up the pathway, Patrick points to a towering rhododendron on the right side of a ravine, the size and scale of the plant larger than my terrace house in London. Noting that it's been there since 1866, my mouth drops open at the wonder of longevity. He stops to touch a bloom the size of a giant's hand on a tree opposite, remarking that the vibrant pink color reminds him of the "psychedelic Tiddlywinks my mother-in-law wore on her ears when she was alive." And the crowd erupts in laughter once again.

Patrick purposely purports how much he abhors politics. Admits to writing poetry as a method of dealing with authorities.

He stops walking, turns around, and extemporaneously recites a poem as if talking to the branches overhead. Disparaging rhymes about a troublesome politician raise a few eyebrows. We've only just met Patrick a few moments before the tour began, but according to ancestry.com, the branches on my mother's side of our ancestral tree have been entwined with the Penningtons' for more than a thousand years.

As H investigates our ancestral roots, we are pleasantly surprised to learn that relatives left remains from a wealth of research, digging around all the way back to three-digit years. Linked to Isaac Pennington, born in 1584, an English politician who sat in the House of Commons from 1640 to 1653, served as Lord Mayor of London in 1642, and was a prominent member of Oliver Cromwell's government. A staunch Puritan, Isaac was present for the execution of William Laud, a churchman appointed by the Archbishop of Canterbury, killed for theological beliefs differing from the norm of the day. A little detail about my genealogy that I don't often insert into conversations with British Anglicans.

But I wouldn't miss this garden tour from the mischievous man who knows every crevice, branch, and bloom on this loamy expanse of history. He's telling us how to live a good story by being himself with every step. Jokes, innuendo, eyebrow-arching comments—he reminds me that blunt honesty spoken in love removes the mirage of the perfected life. It helps to define the landscape for all its panoramic scars and imperfections, to remind us of who we are in the deep underground of the soul.

His slow, confident, methodic steps pressed firmly into ancient soil tell me that age and circumstance are mutually exclusive to calling. That to live a good story means understanding who wrote it. That there will be hills and valleys along the way, but they don't change the course written in the Book of Life with your name on the spine. Even when taking a detour from time to time.

As people parade through his home, see his clothes cloaked over a radiator in the bedroom, interrupt his bowl of pea soup on the picnic table of the public eatery, he responds to each person with dignity and a broad smile. To sacrifice time, reputation, and privacy for the sake of something greater than yourself is the kind of story that sticks to your skin like honey. It tastes sweet and leaves you longing for more.

When I look out the window, past wisteria vines hanging on the stone wall, over the wide expanse of verdant hills, manicured box hedge, and a rainbow of flowers waving in the wind, standing inside the castle where my ancestors once lived, what has been sustained for generations to enjoy is how I imagine God envisioning our future. When I think back upon my childhood, tearful and afraid of what was lurking just outside the doorway, had I projected a future based on the uncertainty of those years, I would've missed the certainty of God's arms carrying me across an ocean now. I would've missed the certainty of being named by him with abundance. And perhaps, "Now we see things imperfectly, like puzzling reflections in a mirror, but then we will see everything with perfect clarity. All that I know now is partial and incomplete, but then I will know everything completely, just as God now knows me completely" (1 Corinthians 13:12 NLT).

Children learn to recognize the name given to them by hearing it spoken repeatedly. A name can be used as a cuss word in anger or an endearment. When uncertainty calls your name, what do you hear? *I am loved* or *I am damned? I am salvation* or *God is my salvation?* Because translation determines perspective.

Practice ADORATION TO REVEAL FALSE NARRATIVES

Have some fun and Google the etymology of your name. How does the meaning of your name reflect who you are?

What are the words that characterize God for you?

Read Miriam's song of deliverance in Exodus 15 as a prayer of adoration. What words stand out in terms of describing God's character and nature?

What are the words you are using to name current uncertainties right now?

Read Exodus 34:6 and adore God's attributes. How does adoration change your perspective regarding current unknowns?

When was the first time you remember feeling brave and confident?

How is that memory naming you now?

How has your interpretation of the state of the world been slanted by false reports from voices of giants? How does adoration change the voice and the narrative?

How have you discarded God's power by reacting in fear?

ELEVEN

Gratitude Brings Focus to the Blur of Uncertainty

Every morning as I turn kale and blueberries
upside down in a magic cup,
swimming in almond milk

My mind returns to a kitchen in Kansas
where a supersized granite island holds
an altar of remembrance,
three friends scattered.

I ache to add one more day
on a string of five.
Instead, I sigh into the quiet.

A RARE SUMMER day in June, the air feels like Arizona heat
melding with Texas humidity. Gauzy dresses stick to skin and
rivulets of sweat drip down the spine. Languid Londoners are
seated on trains, buses, and tubes, frozen because moving equals
a hot flash.

Sash windows are open from ledge to top on three levels of the house, flanked by motionless curtains. Flower boxes boast bent heads on frail stems. Fans pulled from the garage are dusted off in preparation for the arrival of visitors, two longtime friends hailing from Kansas and California. After they pull suitcases from a black cab into the house, we choose to sit in the garden and sip cold drinks, fanning ourselves with laughter.

My first memorable encounter with Kelly and LuAnn was in the hallway of a retreat center in northern Arizona more than two decades ago. Coveting the Brighton purse hanging over LuAnn's shoulder connected us like a dog on a leash breaking the ice between neighbors. But it was my terrible faux pas that solidified our friendship.

Standing up from sitting in a chair, prepped to make an announcement to retreat attendees, Kelly and LuAnn sit cross-legged on the floor at my feet. As women's ministry leader of the megachurch sponsoring the event, I extended permission for revealing wedding albums I asked the gals to bring beforehand, as an opening for cultivating new friendships. But what I heard at my feet was giggling and what I saw was empty laps instead of conversation centered on photos. "I couldn't decide which marriage album I should bring," said Kelly, triggering contagious laughter between us.

Divorce and remarriage hadn't even occurred to me when I asked women to bring wedding albums on a spiritual retreat. I know, how naïve! And insensitive. Instead of flipping through pages of photos, I heard each of Kelly and LuAnn's stories and discerned character and nature through facial expressions. Honesty and laughter have infused our friendship since the beginning, fostering health and vitality each time we reconnect. We were once intercepted by a stranger in the aisle of Marshalls while shopping together, each handed a business card with a request, "The next time you all get together, call me. You know how to have fun!"

Now an ocean separates me from intimate friends in the U.S., and I rattle around a terrace house in London holding an ache only being known like this can fill. We are not the same age, but navigating similar stages of life in tandem, currently the only women in houses with a husband and son. Our daughters have all flown the nest.

A few minutes into conversation, Kelly and LuAnn are pulling items from suitcases wrapped in colored tissue paper. Along with American products—bars of Crisco, chili seasoning, and magic sponges—there are gifts selected thoughtfully, including my first leather backpack purse—black Calvin Klein with a gold zipper—large enough to carry my Canon EOS. I could show you a trail of jewelry in drawers, appliances in cabinets, books on shelves, paintings on walls, and photos documenting dinners and trips over the years leading back to the generosity of Kelly and LuAnn. Shiny gifts and lavish experiences I could never afford while we live on a meager income, after taking a 75 percent pay cut to fulfill a Macedonian call in London. But the greatest gift received each time we meet is their love and unceasing belief in me.

Days later, we tire of Googling air-conditioned restaurants and sites, and shift from urban scrawl to the quiet charm of the English countryside, anticipating the relief of an air-conditioned train taking us to Chipping Camden for a short respite at Denton's Long House. But the hope of cooling off wilts when warm air blows through open windows. Broken air-conditioning turns anticipation somnolent, as if we are all in a hazy dream longing to wake up, for the entire two-hour journey. Depleted, we enter the house, abandon suitcases in bedrooms, and lie down on the cold marble floor of the entryway, feeling sybaritic, as if we are children making imaginary snow angels. Giggles ensue, reviving our heat-induced malaise.

The next morning, I awaken to the coo of doves on the roof, a breeze cooling the house, and a sentence trailing through first thoughts. *I want you to experience life and not just endure it.*

Since arriving in England, scarcity and survival mentality result as my family lives below what Americans would consider the poverty line. But I am unaware that the fear of scarcity has shifted into an identity, until I hear myself talk to intimate friends. Verbalizing fear about staying current on monthly bills, inability to help Murielle replace a car after an accident, imminent university tuition fees for Harrison, I realize I'm unpacking a litany of lack due to the disparity between need and numbers on a paycheck.

When it comes to finances, what I know in my heart about the faithfulness of God and what comes out of my mouth are two different things. And the honesty of trusted friends holds me accountable. But what they don't know is that Yahweh had already been calling me out, before crawling out of bed; before we gathered for tea, warm croissants, and conversation in the kitchen.

A few days earlier, while ruminating on the story of Ruth gleaning in the fields of Boaz, I sensed God highlighting the story in the Bible as a lesson. *You've been gleaning like Ruth for most of your life, and now you must stop. How foolish it would be if Ruth were still gleaning after she married Boaz. You have a Kingsman Redeemer who looks after your needs and desires.*

Waking up at Long House, pondering Scriptures, the daily reading was a similar thread in the same conversation, stitching together some Fatherly discipline, answers from Scripture for worry prayers I wasn't even aware I was praying. It all added up to the theme of focusing on what I lack instead of his presence—what I have right in front of me. As I read the story of Hannah grieving the closure of her womb, my heart is pierced by conviction.

But Hannah answered, "No, my lord, I am a woman troubled in spirit. I have drunk neither wine nor strong drink, but I have been pouring out my soul before the LORD. Do not regard your servant as a worthless woman, for all along I have been speaking out of my great anxiety and vexation." Then Eli answered, "Go in peace, and the God of Israel grant your petition that you have made to him" (1 Samuel 1:15–17 ESV).

As Hannah sought God's face, lamenting what she lacked in the unfulfilled dream of experiencing motherhood, an epiphany resulted. Once she realized she'd been speaking out of anxiety and vexation rather than faith and trust in God's providence, he set her free to bear children. He remembered her. And I had an epiphany at the kitchen table about doing the same thing, speaking from anxiety and vexation rather than choosing faith in his ability to be our Provider.

What was coming out of my mouth was in direct opposition to what I knew in my heart. It was as if, in that moment sitting across from my Elis—Kelly and Luann—a divine finger pressed Stop on words replaying out of my mouth, the same voice I was hearing *ad nauseam* but couldn't manage to turn off by myself. In that moment, I was made open to receive abundance and freed from being closed off by the fear of scarcity, he remembered me too. *I want you to experience life and not just endure it.*

What are you hearing yourself say that you know in your heart isn't true? What is God providing that fear is blinding you to? How might anxiety and vexation from what you lack be keeping you from release into God's abundance? God wants you to experience life and not just endure it. He watches over you in the wilderness. You will lack nothing, says Deuteronomy 2:7.

God wants you to *experience* life and not just *endure* it.

Trials often precede abundance.

> For you, God, tested us; you refined us like silver. You brought us into prison and laid burdens on our backs. You let people ride over our heads; we went through fire and water, but you brought us to a place of abundance.
>
> Psalm 66:10–12

An earlier psalm (12:6) draws a parallel between God's word and silver "tried" seven times—heated up and dross skimmed for impurities that come to the surface until the refiner can see his face reflected in the shine of pure silver. In the same way a refiner knows how long to heat up the silver, God knows how long we can live in the heat of hardship before it changes us into something ugly. His eyes are fixed on your frame, making sure the trial isn't too hot and the dross is removed from your heart in order that his image can be clearly reflected through your life. Interrupting that process prolongs the work of the Artisan on the masterpiece he is creating that is *you*.

As migrants, my family endures many trials—separation, disorientation, scarcity, poverty, fear, and disappointment. And the seed of *not enough* that was planted early on germinates, leaving shoots of anxiety and vexation in all the places where I've lived, even before London. Gratitude pulls the weeds from the landscape of uncertainty, refining perspective and making space for faith to flourish. In capturing a million intimate gifts, we discern how his face has been shining upon us, even amid the cloud cover of anxiety.

A small sampling from a very long list: An old friend sends skin care products I've longed to try for years but never verbalize to anyone. Another friend leaves behind two tickets for a musical when her trip to London is suddenly cut short, making a rare date night possible for H and me. When summer travel to the family cottage in Canada isn't possible from London, a saint provides a plane ticket for Murielle to fly to the cottage to be with her grandma. And another unexpected financial gift allows H, Harrison, and me to take a week of holiday in Cornwall. Signed books written by author friends in the U.S. push through the mail slot along with plain envelopes holding freshly printed sterling, sent anonymously on numerous occasions, often at exact moments of desperation. Another friend pays for services at a hair salon, cut and color every few months for years.

"The face of Jesus is a face that belongs to us the way our past belongs to us. It is a face that we belong to if only as to the one face out of the past that has perhaps had more to do with the shaping of our present than any other," writes Frederick Buechner.[1] God's face has been shining upon you and me since we took our first breath and slurped our first milk shake. As I look up, I see a gray veil parting, his face shining in sunlight pouring through the stained-glass windows of my church. His countenance flames in leaves turning gold and crimson, creating contrast with historic British architecture. Intercessory prayers of faithful friends I've yet to see face-to-face illuminate his love and belonging through epistolary relationships.

To speak from anxiety and vexation seems such an ingratitude as I take account of the times his extravagant love has been poured out. But when that ominous feeling returns, of being left to fend for myself during trials and tribulations, I recite a litany of abundance, and revelation results. Walking to the tube station, careening past the homeless and business suits, the recitation of gifts fills an empty womb with hopefulness of new things yet to be birthed.

Thank you, Lord, for a warm house, full refrigerator, wardrobe holding choices, running water, and a cozy bed to lay upon. For my faithful husband, healthy kids, and for bringing us to London, the place of my heart. Thank you that I can see, touch, smell, and taste. That my legs and feet allow for travel unhindered from place to place. And generous friends who offer words of encouragement and unconditional love as reminders that you are listening to my prayers.

Peregrinatio defies human wisdom. To the world, it looks foolish, but for the one who discerns the voice of God, the life of a peregrini is the truest way to live in freedom. Trust beyond the tangible and concrete; beyond what the mind comprehends logically and make God the focal point in the *bokeh* of your circumstances. Bokeh (pronounced BOH-kay) comes from the Japanese word *boke*, meaning blur or haze. In photography, bokeh is defined as "the way the lens renders out-of-focus points of light." A shallow depth of field is used to blur the background of the photo, making the subject look sharp while everything else in the frame takes on a soft, indistinct halo. Bokeh creates an aesthetically pleasing capture. Spiritually, the more Christ becomes the focal point, our uncertainties blur in the background, creating a soft receptive posture that is pleasing to him.

Searching for the certainty of God's presence is an act of surrender, a relinquishment of the need to figure everything out as comfort for anxiety. And surrender sets you free from self-limiting beliefs, releasing the Holy Spirit as a guide into truth. "He will not speak on his own; he will speak only what he hears, and he will tell you what is yet to come" (John 16:12–13).

Ungratefulness sets in when I search for certainty through the lens of what I lack instead of the abundance right where I am. The voice of shame results in finger pointing; pointing at myself, others, and God for not being or doing enough. Ultimately, a lack of gratitude is rooted in striving for your worth and value outside of God, motivated by the fear of being unlovable.

"You cannot see my face, for no one may see me and live" (Exodus 33:20). God utters those words to Moses during the Exodus, and they seem uncaring, distant, like God turning the lens to bokeh Moses. I can't hear the intention in God's voice audibly, but what I know is this: By the time God says, "You cannot see my face," Moses had encountered his voice of friendship from a burning bush and his voice of power during plagues in Egypt. He listened to God voicing battle plans against enemies, dictating the Ten Commandments, creating blueprints for the tabernacle, and giving instructions for transporting the Ark of the Covenant. He heard the angry voice of discipline after the Israelites grumbled and the voice of compassion when God relented.

Moses didn't need to see God's face because he was discerning direction by listening. And just like Moses, we discern the future, not in what we see but in hearing God's voice. Auditory acuity lends courage to live differently, as a peregrini rather than a pawn in the chaos of uncertainty. "Faith comes from hearing the message, and the message is heard through the word about

Christ" (Romans 10:17). Belief creates bravery for what seems beyond us.

When God tells Moses, "I will do the very thing you have asked, because I am pleased with you and I know you by name" (Exodus 33:17), I like to think he didn't have to use Moses' name during conversations because of the sacrament of presence practiced between them. It is his voice that leads, shapes, protects, rescues, disciplines, and woos us toward spiritual, emotional, and physical health. "I form light and create darkness; I make *well-being* and create calamity; I am the LORD, who does all these things" (Isaiah 45:7 ESV, emphasis added).

The Exodus story tells us the Lord spoke to Moses face-to-face like a friend, yet he couldn't make eye contact without dire consequences. Lack of eye contact from God in your circumstances isn't an offense or an unloving dismissive, but protection, an opportunity to experience deeper relationship with him. An opening to declare like Moses—*Now show me your glory*—when what you see and what you know are in opposition. Because God is trustworthy when he says, "I will cause all my goodness to pass in front of you" (Exodus 33:19). *I want you to experience life and not just endure it.*

While I am calculating how my life should look, projecting the future based on today's circumstances, I miss the goodness of God right in front of me. We can insist on concrete assurances as a measuring tool for security, yet what we seek might be the death of us if we were to capture a small glimpse of it. Mystery is protection, not ambivalence. And specificity is applicable when it is good for us: Stand here on this rock next to me. When I pass by, I'll cover you with my hand. When I safely pass, I will remove my hand and you will see my back. But my face must not be seen.

I am with you.
I will protect you.
Clarity comes with distance.
I know what is best for you.

God has your back even though you cannot see the whites of his eyes in your circumstances. Becoming familiar with Voice in Scripture helps identify his whereabouts in the heat of circumstances. And prayer is an intimate conversation, not a monologue for spectators. "He did not say anything to them without using a parable. But when he was alone with his own disciples, he explained everything" (Mark 4:34). It is only in intimacy and vulnerability that Jesus reveals to us what is hidden beyond the headlines. And with some practice, your voice will ring like goodness to someone like my virtual friend JodyBeth, desperate when the situation looks anything but good.

"A SEASON OF uncertainty has blown into our family," writes JodyBeth in response to a blog post I published. She explains that the company where her husband is employed has gone into reorganization. Nine people are now vying for five positions. Her husband's acceptance of one of those positions will result in a significant drop in pay as well as lowering his job title. Their options translate as deeply disappointing rather than God working all things together for their good.

"As I walked away from my husband telling me he's ready to find a new job, fear welled up within me," JodyBeth admits.

I learn this isn't their first experience with uncertainty of this magnitude. In seventeen years of marriage, their current scenario marks the third time with global layoffs. The last two resulted in job loss; more than twelve months of unemployment each time.

"I was afraid until I read what you wrote about Moses," Jody-Beth continues. "Okay, God, now show us your glory! I cannot begin to express to you how profound those words are to me right now. They have shifted something within me. From the land of fear to the land of the Father. Still, uncertainty looms with the threat of joblessness, but I am not alone. I have a Father who wants to reveal his glory to me for my benefit, and through me for the benefit of others. He loves me and he knows the plan for us, so I can rest in that assurance."

That epiphany for JodyBeth sounds too simple, doesn't it? Just believe God loves you and everything will be fine. Enter uncertainty and become disoriented at best. You feel vulnerable, alone, disappointed, and haunted by emptiness. For some, no familiar signposts offer pathways toward hopeful conclusions. For others, all the signs from the past are plentiful, triggering anxiety and the fear of repeating undesirable seasons. The less we know about the future, the more anxious we become. How can you believe God is working all things together for your good, when it looks like he's left the building?

Two weeks later, an update slides quietly into my inbox from JodyBeth. Eddie is scheduled to meet with his boss without details as to the subject matter. Her mind is whirling with what-ifs, and her heart is a hurricane of anxiety.

"I confess my stomach is in knots," admits JodyBeth. "To ask God to reveal his glory is accepting that it probably involves a hard road ahead. Does he get more glory in the easy or hard road? I keep asking myself this question. Because I don't want a hard road, Shelly. But I do want Jesus and I want him more than an easy life (I think I threw up a little in my mouth typing that!). Show me your glory is not for the faint of heart! I'm struggling. Please pray for us."

I do pray for Eddie, JodyBeth, and their children. Fervently. And I suggest she ask a few trusted friends to pray with them too. Even Moses had Aaron and Hur holding up his arms to prevail in battle with the Amalekites. We cannot come to clarity on our own. We cannot win spiritual battles without help. The way to clarity is through the complexities of life.

Later that day, I receive another email from JodyBeth summing up the outcome of our prayers in three simple lines. "Eddie's last day is May 11. I can't even think now. . . . Thank you for your prayers. You have no idea what a gift that is."

You might be asking, *How can an answer to prayer be a gift when the result is job loss? How can silence be God's good answer for uncertainty that could have devastating consequences?* The gift is not in the outcome; it is in knowing you are not alone. The answer you didn't know you need to uncertainty is the assurance that you are loved; God's presence is with you because you belong to him. He assures, "I will personally go with you, Moses, and I will give you rest—everything will be fine for you" (Exodus 33:14 NLT). Go ahead, insert your name for Moses and claim that promise for yourself right now.

After the initial shock, JodyBeth writes me again the next day, describing the atmosphere of her heart as "being buoyed on a bubble" with "the peace that passes all understanding" that Paul writes about in his letter to the Philippians. But they also wonder when the other shoe will drop. When will the bubble of calm burst and the unknowns deflate the faith that is keeping them afloat right now?

They ask a few friends and family members to lend prayer support, admitting that they need reminders of the truth when fear will eventually cause situational spiritual amnesia. Will you wander for the love of God? Or will you wander into self-sufficiency? These are the questions God asks us in times of uncertainty.

Five months pass until I hear from JodyBeth again. Then an unexpected follow-up email causing my mouth to drop open when I read it. "The day we received Eddie's last severance check, he signed an offer with a local company, and he began work two weeks later. God's impeccable timing and provision have left us shaking our heads with tear-filled eyes." She assesses the third round of layoffs a series of events they would've never asked for but ultimately lead to fulfilling the desire of their hearts.

"Eddie has come home daily with a smile on his face, loving his job, enjoying co-workers, feeling appreciated by his superiors. It's been nine years since any of those things have happened. It's shake-your-head crazy, laugh-out-loud good, impeccable timing, mind-blowing grace."

Imagine my surprise when her next paragraph begins, "I sit in tears now, because I sit in regret.

"I wish that during this season I had trusted God more. I wish I had believed him more. He has proven so many times to me that he is trustworthy and faithful. He is good and good to me. I have walked with God for almost thirty years and yet, I still had not managed to rest fully in his character and Word when our world seemed to be falling apart. I knew I could trust him, and yet I lived with mixed anxiety and stress, wondering how long this time would be. What would I do? How would I manage?"

JodyBeth echoes what so many of us experience on the backside of uncertainty. The exhale of relief that comes in the beauty of fulfilled promises also holds up a mirror reflecting the idol of self-sufficiency. "I missed out on knowing him more because I was absorbed with my circumstances. That brings regret because my trust was misplaced," explains JodyBeth. "The lesson I learned is whatever the world throws at me, he sees me. He sees me through, all the way Home."

Perhaps you are blind to the evidence of God's love in your current situation; *I want you to experience life and not just endure it* seems like a promise for everyone else but you. *Now show me your glory* is a challenge worthy of taking; a declaration of belief in the unseen and not yet, because he sees what is hidden and knows your name. You have favor with him.

In the classic book *The Screwtape Letters*, C. S. Lewis creates a theory called the *Law of Undulation*, a series of peaks and valleys that are experienced as common to humanity. He describes us as having two parts: the spirit directed to the eternal, and the bodies, passions, and imaginations that experience continual change—"for to be in time means to change."

"Their nearest approach to constancy, therefore, is undulation—the repeated return to a level from which they repeatedly fall back, a series of troughs and peaks," writes Lewis.[2]

In short, our desires and longings—in relationships, work, play, and rest—go up and down. What was rich and lively

Dull and dry times
we *experience*
in life are not a result
of enemy attack
but a natural
rhythm of life.

can quickly become numbness and poverty. We can feel guilty about revisiting a dreary trough after time celebrating on the peak. But Lewis makes a case that the dull and dry times we experience in life are not a result of enemy attack but a natural rhythm of life.

Sheep typically like to travel in a straight line, and this can cause real problems when the shepherd calls out to the herd across a trough. Their trust in each other can lead them right off a cliff or into deep valleys where they get stuck. As prevention from getting into trouble, the shepherd guides the herd in a zigzag pattern, undulating down a hillside. The ups and downs of life keep us dependent on Christ. Why do sheep follow their shepherd? Because they've practiced hearing and identifying the voice of love. Be wary of translating a trough—a time of great unknowing in circumstances of uncertainty—as God's abandonment, only to assume dependence on self. That can be dangerous to your soul and keep you from God's rest.

The enemy of your soul remains vigilant about making good use of the valleys along the way. He distorts God-given pleasures to fulfill a selfish desire, a counterfeit comfort that boasts peak experience and promises a lack of trough. "An ever-increasing craving for an ever-diminishing pleasure is the formula" for keeping you in a constant state of unrest.

The Israelites were freed from captivity (peak) only to grumble a short while later about boredom with manna (trough) and a craving for meat. The desire for something they did not have created blindness to what was right in front of them—God's presence. Craving what you want but cannot seem to grasp creates cycles of chronic restlessness. And prolonged unrest leads to anxiety.

When the Lord passes in front of Moses, he doesn't call out Moses' name as a gesture of assurance. Rather, God called out his own name: "Yahweh! The Lord! The God of compassion and mercy! I am slow to anger and filled with unfailing love and faithfulness. I lavish unfailing love to a thousand generations" (Exodus 34:6–7 NLT).

Initially, uncertainty can translate as being damned. Damned to fail, to lose, to be overlooked, forgotten, outcast, exiled, bereft, adrift, and doomed to live a life sentence of hardship. That's what I used to think until I discovered uncertainty is less about me and more about the I AM Moses met on the mountain. God spoke to Moses face-to-face, as a friend sitting cross-legged on the floor (Exodus 33:11), flipping through a photo album. He calls Abraham his friend (Isaiah 41:8) and refers to Job as his friend when talking to Satan (Job 42:7–8). God leaves trails of abundance, all the gifts leading back to his enduring friendship with you (John 15:15). Rehearsing the truth in gratitude changes a distant God into an intimate friend, one who longs for you to *experience life and not just endure it.*

Practice GRATITUDE IN THE WILDERNESS OF SCARCITY

Are you experiencing life or enduring it right now?

What are you hearing yourself say that you know isn't true in your heart?

Is there disparity between the truth and vexation for you? Take a few minutes of silence to repent and ask for forgiveness.

Practice gratitude daily. What are you grateful for that might normally be overlooked? Make a list you can look back upon during times of uncertainty.

How does gratitude change your mood and outlook?

Who are the people that will remind you of what is true?

Who are the people waiting for you to be a truth-teller amid their uncertainty?

Approach every day as an opportunity to spend time with your intimate friend, Jesus. How does being deeply loved and fully known change the way you respond to the unknown?

How can you pass on the gift of his friendship to others?

TWELVE

Remembering Restores Certainty

There will come a time
when all the places you wandered
will become the places you can only travel
in your mind.

Retrace previous pavements,
sore feet a distant memory
rather than exclamation
of present reality.

H AND I neglect ordering a keepsake wedding album documenting our big day. In that admission, I realize I have increased the severity of the faux pas that happened on my watch as a ministry leader. It highlights the ridiculousness of asking women to bring something to a spiritual retreat that I don't have myself. But it's not as bad as it sounds.

After the wedding dress was purchased, menu created, tennis court tented, tables and chairs rented, flowers ordered, Jewish folk dancers booked, and photographer settled, the budget was depleted. Perhaps it's more honest to say that a wedding album wasn't a *priority* in the budget. But our photographer became an agent of redemption when he gifted us with a sequence of proofs; hundreds of 3x5 photos in one of those vertical albums with plastic sleeves, three per page. At the time, that white album with gold embellishments provided proof of wedding vows and an adequate keepsake for marking a new season of life.

Stored in the original white cardboard box with gold lid, the album is tucked away among boxes of china and mementos in a storage unit in the United States. But a glossy 8x10 ordered by Murielle's namesake, H's grandmother, was inherited when she passed away and transported to London after the funeral.

We can say that memories choose us, but that's telling a half-truth. I believe God is selectively choosing snapshots from the heap of mental frames captured, highlighting intimacies that are important for each of us. Memories that return repeatedly among the infinitude of details that make up our lives are often undocumented by photos or scribbling in a journal.

For instance, I did not snap a photo of my grandmother's smiling facial expression as she lay prostrate in the bed next to mine during our summer vacation. But her loving, kind face captured that day is memorable and returns to mind often. A few hours after making silent eye contact that warm sunny day at the Lake of the Ozarks, my grandmother admitted she was having an angina attack. A smile amid suffering communicates more than a glossy 8x10.

Eating an after-school snack outside at the home of a child-hood friend, I watch with curiosity as she twirls in the rain. Arms raised toward heaven, she exclaims, "It's a God-rain because the sun is out!" Like a lone audience member critiquing a dramatic interpretation of rain falling on a sunny day, I can't remember the name of the actress or credit the writing of her monologue to a Scripture verse, but I recall how the sky shimmered pink-gold raining diamonds; how her declaration provoked independent investigation into truth over assigning someone's truth as my own. When it rains on a sunny day in London, that random memory comes flooding back to me with a message *Stay attentive to Light shining through the unexpected.*

I'm not a trained psychologist, but I believe our recycled memories carry hints to the way we are created to bring ourselves into the world. They reveal what we do when the pressure is on and when time is idle; how we respond to something new and how we translate uncertainty in the heat of disappointment. Our memories illustrate courage and weakness amid adversity, and how we define beauty, home, and belonging.

The wildly popular television series *This Is Us* is impacting a whole generation of viewers by showing how our past informs, impairs, and intuits our future. Whatever stage of life we find ourselves in, the stories depicted through a family of characters hold up a mirror to our brokenness. Scenes from the past shown simultaneously with present day allow us to see how key experiences in the parents' marriage and home life for each of their children have the power to impact them as adults.

Much like the unique stories we live out daily, three siblings in *This Is Us* navigate the challenges of adulthood (marriage, parenting, relationships, career, identity), and the flashbacks make their current trials, difficulties, and responses clear and relatable to viewers. Wouldn't it be fabulous if we could rewind the reels of life and watch our story unfold in real time? Would we be kinder to ourselves? More accepting of our weaknesses and frailties? Would we show self-compassion more easily knowing why we are prone to stumble over the same issues? How might we translate and respond to uncertainty differently? *This Is Us* is a

> Our *memories* illustrate courage and weakness amid *adversity,* and how we define beauty, home, and *belonging.*

weekly reminder in the living rooms of homes across the world that where we come from matters, but the disruptions of life do not define the success or failure of our future.

In her famous TED Talk, Brené Brown communicates how our stories of worthiness, of being enough, begin in our first families—what we learn about ourselves and how we learn to engage with the world as children—and set a course that either will require us to spend a significant portion of our life fighting to reclaim our self-worth, or will give us hope, courage, and resilience for our journey. Perhaps that's our greatest choice in life—fighting for self-worth or surrendering to Hope. As I look back over the early frames in my personal "This Is Us" story, I capture Love blowing through the open windows of my childhood and Light settling over old narratives, rewriting them as new. Hope carried me when I couldn't stand on my own, and later, hope came in the way of gatekeepers opening doors for H and me to walk through.

MARRIED ON MAY 5, 1990, H and I forever marked our union by Cinco de Mayo, a Mexican holiday celebrated in Phoenix annually with parades, food, and dancing. Observed by Mexicans to commemorate the Mexican army's victory over the French Empire at the Battle of Puebla on May 5, 1862. But for Americans, it's an excuse to overindulge in tamales, chili rellenos, refried beans, and margaritas made with salt and fresh lime juice. For H and me, no excuse for forgetting our anniversary.

Nothing on our wedding reception menu resembled flour tortillas, chili con carne, or burritos. Looking back, I think that might've been an egregious error. When pressed about what we miss the most about living in a different culture, outside of our daughter, eating Mexican food is our number-one answer. We have been known to import tamales from Arizona for a traditional Christmas Eve dinner in London.

Mexican food, a desert landscape of palm trees and saguaro, dry heat, three hundred days of sunshine a year—all made up the environment that began our union. But a few months after signing a one-year lease on a condo, we began wandering through the wilderness of the desert. H had just graduated with a Bachelor of Architecture from the University of Southern California, but the job market was a graveyard for architects, dried up due to a downturn in the economy. Days before our honeymoon I lost my advertising sales job and days after returning to Phoenix, H was let go from a struggling architecture firm. Those early losses in the way of unemployment affirmed an inkling we were both discerning about next steps.

Weeks later, during a Sunday morning worship service, our pastor walked off the platform during a song, joining H and me where we were standing with eyes closed and palms up in surrender. And he whispered words of discernment about a ministry leadership gift he was observing. Words that confirmed an inkling about ministry being our vocation as a couple, not a side gig. Instead of constructing buildings, God was preparing H to be a spiritual architect, envisioning structures for church planting beyond bricks and mortar that allow the kingdom to flourish.

We walked out of the church, into the parking lot, holding hands in silence under a canopy of sun and marble blue sky. Climbing inside the car, as our eyes met, wells glimmering with pools of tears released onto cheeks and dripped on our chests. Hanging heads over laps, we wept, thanking God for direction. Our peregrinatio journey as a married couple was just beginning. Could this be the unique Promised Land we envisioned on our honeymoon?

At the recommendation of the pastor whom I heard preach the first Sunday I arrived in Phoenix, H enrolled in a Master of Divinity program at the Church of God School of Theology in Cleveland, Tennessee. Packing up our new home into boxes, the landlord graciously released us from the one-year lease with his blessing. We sold H's Volvo to a friend, giving us just enough to fill the gas tanks on two vehicles, rent a moving van, and provide first and last month's rent on an apartment. The church agreed to help pay for H's tuition, but without jobs, we had no idea where or how we might live; we just knew we were called to wander for the love of God to a place that was foreign to us. Lifting final boxes into the moving van, our progress was interrupted by the phone ringing. H reported that the call was from the theological college confirming his acceptance into the master's program.

"That's good, since we are already packed and ready to move across the country!" I laughed.

Thankfully, there wasn't time to scout out the land beforehand, because like the Israelites, we might have turned around and returned to the desert of Phoenix. We were trusting that milk and honey awaited us, but when we landed, nothing about the place or the church culture that founded the School of Theology was desirable to our sensibilities.

While H was taking notes during lectures, I worked as a receptionist at a highly successful chiropractor's office, scheduling hundreds of patients for treatments and adjustments. It wasn't uncommon to witness patients arriving on stretchers, unable to walk without pain, leaving the clinic and walking pain free. Dr. Free (yes, that really is his name!) is a man of God who prays for his patients with their permission. And we all witnessed the power of God's healing on the regular. Dr. Free worked tirelessly with a Cheshire smile frozen on his face daily, as if he knew something we were all remiss to claim. During a break from seeing patients, he rested his elbows on the counter, smiled, and kindly asked, "What do you feel God is calling you to do in ministry?"

Replying sheepishly, I admitted that H and I felt God was asking us to reach people of wealth with the Gospel. Wealthy people need the Good News too, but the vision sounds haughty and presumptive as I hear the words come out of my mouth. Who wouldn't enjoy ministering to wealthy people?! Heat rises into my cheeks as I hear the hilarity in the statement, but the conviction continues rumbling in my heart to this day.

Two years later, beginning the final leg in H's theological degree, an opportunity with Youth With A Mission (YWAM) comes into our purview with potential for satisfying hours needed to complete the program. A mentoring internship with Floyd McClung, international director of YWAM at the time. The opportunity was unconventional in terms of what the School of Theology considered as ministry practice, but they allowed it. We applied and were accepted into the pilot program. Our hearts soared with thoughts of a new peregrinatio journey.

Converging with kindreds from all over the world, we moved to Idyllwild, California, into a summer house, where in the winter we cooked dinner in coats and gloves, and awakened to frost gleaming on the inside of windows. Humbled by complete dependence upon the financial support of friends and family for food, logs, and rent, there wasn't enough left over in the budget for electric heating. At the same time, we received a letter from the theological college including a delinquent tuition bill, alerting us to the disappointing news that our church in Phoenix had stopped paying H's school fees.

Survival became a higher priority than H finishing his degree. At the time, it was as if H was repeating my dad's history, only three hours away from graduating with a master's degree when the progress is halted by a powerful gatekeeper.

Refusal to make an opening for us evokes frustration and anger, much like I imagine happening with Balaam when his donkey halts, refusing to move past the unseen angel blocking the path. The "ass" refused to budge, and we don't know if we want to lament, cry, pound our fists, or give up. We had arrived at the *pons asinorum*, the ass's bridge.

"The ancient world used the term to describe the moment a geometry student is asked to define the isosceles triangle. Suddenly, the going gets rough. The student begins to think that studying geometry is not worth the effort. The ass he is riding—his will—is refusing to cross the bridge and the student doesn't know how to cross it any other way. The changes required of the student for continuing the journey seem too great. He just wants to quit.

"The *pons asinorum* is actually a neurological barrier. It is the point at which new synaptic connections must be formed to accommodate the increased mental traffic. It's a part of what we now call neuroplasticity, the brain's amazing ability to adjust to the new demands placed on it. However, this process of brain reorganization is taxing. When we start crossing the *pons asinorum* everything in us wants to quit and return to our accustomed life."

Rather than allow a gatekeeper to hold our future hostage, we arrive at *pons asinorum* and something amazing takes place. Prone toward problem-solving as a reaction to uncertainty, my heart opens to mystery, crossing the bridge from fear into peace that is unexplainable.

The Israelites arrive in the Desert of Zin, and everything seems to be crumbling around them once again. Miriam passes away and the water supply dries up. And no water means Moses and Aaron are the objects of grumbling once again. *Why did you bring us here to die in the desert? Why can't we go back to where the water never ran out?* And don't you know that the desert can be a stretch of beach overlooking the ocean if you aren't receiving what you need to survive inner unrest?

The brothers fell facedown at the entrance of the Tent of Meeting and God issued a plan. "Speak to that rock before their eyes and it will pour out its water. You will bring water out of the rock for the community so they and their livestock can drink" (Numbers 20:8). But instead of speaking to the rock, Moses hits the rock with a stick. Water gushes out and thirst for the Israelites is satiated. But Moses and Aaron pay a hefty price for impulsiveness.

God replies, "Because you did not trust in me enough to honor me as holy in the sight of the Israelites, you will not bring this community into the land I give them" (Numbers 20:12).

Like Balaam, did Moses' patience run out? Is that why he hit the rock rather than speaking to it? Or perhaps God's patience with all the grumbling Israelites had finally hit a ceiling? What are we defining as roadblocks that God is providing as protection? What situations are provoking angry outbursts rather than evoking listening for the words of Jesus?

Scholars aren't unified about why Moses hit the rock instead of speaking to it—why God responded with what seems such a harsh discipline. Perhaps keeping those details a mystery from us is God's intention. Because what we can take away from the story of Moses and Balaam—hitting rather than speaking with God-given authority—is that God is the gatekeeper of our lives. He decides which doors will open and close for each of us. That's why we cannot compare someone's open door with our stuck hinges. He appoints and revokes gatekeepers for reasons that remain hidden from public knowledge. And impulsiveness during waiting seasons—taking matters into our own hands—can have detrimental consequences.

We learned of the consequences of selfish ambition in earlier chapters from the story of a group of discontented, grumbling Korahites, who took matters into their own hands and dissolved into the earth as fertilizer. It remains a mystery as to why God elected the Sons of Korah as gatekeepers for the Temple when their tribe was characterized as selfish and untrustworthy. But the Sons of Korah remained faithful to the appointment for centuries.

> The four chief gatekeepers, who were Levites, were entrusted to be over the chambers and the treasures of the house of God. And they lodged around the house of God, for on them lay the duty of watching, and they had charge of opening it every morning.
>
> 1 Chronicles 9:26-27 ESV

Not only were the Sons of Korah in charge of money, opening and closing entrances, and overseeing rooms, but they were also in charge of transporting a portable tabernacle through the wilderness and packing up at a moment's notice. "Whenever the cloud lifted from above the tent, the Israelites set out; wherever the cloud settled, the Israelites encamped. At the LORD's command the Israelites set out, and at his command they encamped" (Numbers 9:17–18). Sometimes the cloud canopied the tabernacle for a few days, and other times a few hours or many months.

From necessity, the Israelites become vigilant cloud watchers, waiting without forecasts about how long or short a stay in one place might be. They are characterized as wanderers rather than those who lay down roots. And I suppose H and I could say the same about ourselves. Since arriving in London, people often ask, "How long will you stay?" And our answer is always the same. We're 100 percent committed to stay forever unless God gives us a sign that it's time to move on. As cloud watchers through the practice of spiritual disciplines, we have learned to discern when grace has lifted, when it's time to pitch our tent in a new place. London is our ninth "campground" in three decades of marriage, and we've been asked the question in each of the previous places we've made home. Our certainty is not in a place, but in God who creates places for us to bring him into the world.

> God isn't as interested in our situational *certainty* as he is about sovereign *perspective*.

In some of the places where we were led, we pleaded for release due to loneliness or lack of belonging; cultural disparity or aversion to the spiritual landscape. We grumbled and complained, often begging God to send us back to the Egypt we created in our minds with nostalgia. But God isn't as interested in our situational certainty as he is about sovereign perspective.

Why would God put the Israelites through all that work of tearing down and pitching camp in a new place, only to land for a few hours? Why all the continual uncertainty in the wilderness when he could've provided the certainty of promise in a few weeks? Why? The answer is a word we are averse to hear: obedience.

During the Exodus journey, to move ahead or lag behind translates as *disobedience*. How do we learn to live in peace when inevitable disruptions happen? We wait on God. Watch for the signs of his presence. Walk through open doors and yield when doors close. If you think having your own personal cloud of certainty would be easier than being vulnerable to the disruptions caused by uncertainty, the Exodus story reveals the opposite. Most of us would love to know exactly when to move and be led to the exact destination God has planned for us next, but instead, he extends the grace of choice. And hopes we'll say yes to wandering with him.

Our cloud lifts and hovers over Tennessee, California, Colorado, and back to Phoenix during the first eight years of marriage. I assume Phoenix is our Promised Land, as the new pastor at Valley Cathedral, Dan Scott, hailing from Nashville, discerns a ministry partnership with us while officiating H's father's funeral. He offers H a position on a large staff at the megachurch, and later, gatekeepers create a huge reduction on the sale of a house adjacent to the church property, making a beautiful home a reality for us in central Phoenix. After living as missionaries on support, a weekly paycheck translates as relief and certainty. But a pregnancy test reveals the arrival of our first child will come before our insurance is activated.

Inquiring about payments with the gynecologist I chose on referral from a trusted source, I explain that the timing of the pregnancy is incongruous with our new insurance plan. "I don't charge pastor's wives for my services. Don't worry about that," he tells me. And his promise carries on when I become pregnant a second time with our son, Harrison.

A few years later, just as workers finish the grout and tile, transforming a koi pond back into to a proper swimming pool in our backyard, we are blindsided when the cloud begins showing signs of lifting again. Individual prayers for H and me intersect in corporate discernment. God is giving us all the familiar signs that he may be wanting us to move again, even though we are content living in Phoenix. Signs that culminate on summer vacation with my dad, Carol, and Sean in Pawleys Island, their traditional vacation spot.

Uncharacteristically, while on vacation, we attend church the first Sunday of our summer respite, and the bishop delivering the sermon spots us seated among the crowd. Intersecting on the lawn, he asks if we might be willing to extend our vacation and visit a church a few hours away in North Carolina. Consider moving to lead All Saints Anglican Church, a vibrant congregation without a pastor, meeting in a strip center next to Hooters. My first thought was the vow I made when we left Tennessee for California: *I will never again make my home in the South.* But we visit and I relent. Once I witness H's shepherd's heart open to the people of Morehead City, I surrender past experience for present possibility.

We sell the house adjacent to the church just as the market begins to turn around, giving us a financial cushion absent in the first years of our marriage. After driving across the country for several days, inhaling the scent of new leather from the seats of our freshly purchased Honda minivan, we pull into the driveway of our new address and survey the blue hydrangea bushes I specifically request from the landscaping company, flowers I could never cultivate in the desert. The builder of the house and scent of wood floors greet us as we walk inside the spacious open floor plan. It's our first experience with making choices about faucets, paint color, moulding, flooring, door handles, and plants growing around the perimeter of our acreage.

We project at least ten years at All Saints but grow restless after three. And I begin wondering if my body has a secret circadian rhythm attached to experiencing new places and people every few years. But H is experiencing unexplainable inner unrest too. The mark of a peregrini is homesickness that never leaves because homesickness is the way home until Christ is satisfied with your journey.

The cloud moves five years later at a most unconventional time, astounding not only us, but those we are leading. On the Sunday morning we consecrate the architectural masterpiece of a new church H helps envision, construct, and fund for All Saints, the visiting bishop offers H a position as director of leadership development for the Anglican Mission in America and quickly promotes him to executive director, helping facilitate healthy church plants in the United States and Canada. We move to Pawleys Island, the place where we enjoy decades of vacations with my parents, a place we never desired to live permanently. We're hopeful to find kindred community elusive to us since leaving Phoenix. But community never happens the way I envision it unfolding.

Instead of drop-ins from friends, impromptu meetups at the beach, shopping with girlfriends, community is cultivated virtually. As I shift from a part-time job as a primary feature writer to writing from passion about my life on a blog, intimate friendships develop in faraway places. Many become gatekeepers who open doors that progress my writing into a global ministry and authoring books.

WHAT I REMEMBER about my wedding day that isn't documented by a sequence of proofs is the French ribbon holding my wedding bouquet together, dyed to match the color of the bridesmaids' dresses. The stems were wet. Hues the color of moving sea shaded by rocks on a sunny day bled onto the champagne silk of the bodice and train. As I held my dad's arm, poised at the entrance of the church, preparing to walk down the aisle toward H, I noticed the stain and realized there was nothing I could do to change the imperfection of that moment. Relationship with Dad wasn't fatherly like it is with H and my children, but he offered compassion, like holding a milk shake with two straws between us. As I walked past rows of pews, I don't remember a single facial expression among hundreds gathered to witness our union that day. I remember not seeing the faces of my grand-parents staring back at me. Grandma was too afraid to fly, and Grandpa feared disappointing her.

Later at the reception, like a voyeur witnessing a pedestrian stumble among crowds in Trafalgar Square, I remember my mother sitting in the corner with her new but short-lived husband whose name I can't remember. Nursing a sore foot and a bruised ego, she was injured when someone's stiletto heel landed inside her shoe during the Jewish folk dancing at the reception, grounding her for the rest of the evening.

THE EXODUS STORY of three siblings—Moses, Aaron, and Miriam—doesn't read as perfectly happy but imperfect, not what we hope for or envision. I've lamented and wept over the Au-thor's choice of ending for them, perhaps because my definition of love is bound by the limits of my perspective. All that time wandering together as a family, experiencing miracles, terrify-ing middles, and celebrations of deliverance, and yet, not one of them would enter the Promised Land. None of them would experience a happy conclusion from forty years of sacrifice and surrender. God's choice seems unfair, unloving in response to the sequence of proofs capturing devotion. But maybe we are missing the point when we rely on a pretty bow to tie chapters of our stories together?

Sometimes grieving a different ending is an appropriate re-sponse. Behold, the landscape of your life has prepared the way, not for amassing wealth but for the rich legacy of hope left for future generations. You may not experience biting into the low-hanging fruit cultivated in the rich soil of your hard work, but you will capture a glimpse of abundance awaiting your children and those you influence for the kingdom. They will pluck and savor from the branch that is yours in the genealogy of God's kingdom. What could be more valuable than the tree of your life flourishing, rooted and nurtured by the intimacy of relationship with the Father? We need a bow to pull back the arrow of hope; releasing the glory of God's presence revealed.

The arrow lands for us in one of the most affluent neighborhoods in London, where we share the love of God with shopkeepers and neighbors, exiles from places around the world. The wealth of our lives, we quickly discover, is not in sterling or dollars, but in the transformation of those who find Jesus.

Two years after landing in London, Harrison is named head boy of Chelsea Academy, and we discern God's presence in a leadership gift emerging. He chooses the University of Lancaster and studies history near the Lakes District, eerily close in proximity to where my English ancestry began. He returns home to London at Christmas, flourishing.

At the same time Harrison is becoming acclimated to living on his own, Murielle makes the courageous choice to move away from friends and familiarity for a fresh start in her birthplace of Phoenix, Arizona, closer to family. Repeating my history, she loads her compact car with possessions, embarking upon her unique peregrinatio journey without a job or peer community in place yet. Driving cross-country alone, Murielle leaves Raleigh, North Carolina, in the winter and arrives on the driveway of her grandmother's house in sunny Phoenix a few days later. She is thriving where God has planted her.

Dad sends a new email with a photo attached, sharing a new memory emerging as he helps Carol decorate the house for Christmas. A memory from before my parents' divorce, while making home in the condo. It's a picture of a tiny ornament, a little angel made from a pipe cleaner with small paper wings, the face drawn with eyes closed detailing fine lashes lying on cheeks. "The ornament has been on every Christmas tree that I have had since you were born. It was saved from your very first Christmas package. Our Christmas decorations are not complete until this goes on the tree."

We are born searching for certainty but begin living when we find the certainty of the Father's love. Uncertain times translate as an "aha!" instead of an "oh no!" because ultimately, the unknown is an opening to give God glory.

Practice PRAYER AND REMEMBRANCE FOR THE WILDERNESS OF FORGETFULNESS

What memories resurface repetitively for you?

What might the memories communicate that you didn't discern initially?

What do the memories say about how God made you to bring yourself into the world?

How is God rewriting false narratives?

Describe a time when you sensed God was lifting a cloud to move you on to the next place.

How did you know it was God moving and not your feelings moving you to act?

Offer a prayer of thanksgiving for the gatekeepers who have opened doors for you in the past.

How can you open the door for someone this week?

How is refusal becoming a roadblock in a relationship? What blessing are you withholding from someone due to stubbornness?

How does grieving a different ending change the way you think about the future?

If you named a goal in chapter 1, is that goal met, exceeded, or forgotten now? Explain.

Epilogue
Certainty Full Circle

A COMMON TRUTH many Christian authors share is that we are often tested by the message God is writing through us. Will the truths and practices penned prove trustworthy, timeless, and true, or will our words be translated irrelevant and trite in the heat of unforeseen circumstances? I pray for the latter.

In March of 2020, I received the first round of edits from my editor on the manuscript that became the book you are now reading. At the same time, I was unexpectedly scheduled for some serious medical tests at a local hospital as the coronavirus pandemic reached England. If I were to measure my uncertainty that month in the same way we assign numbers to hurricanes, life was category 4, everything ramped up as major.

Localized pain on the right side of my abdomen, radiating around to the lower back, resulted in a doctor's order of a CT colonography scheduled at a London hospital. While awaiting the scan, I became breathless walking up stairs, and my left leg suddenly began swelling up while walking around the house. A doctor suggested anxiety as the cause due to the imminent CT. To the doctors in my practice, none of my symptoms seemed connected.

In my heart, I knew something was off even though every ultrasound, blood test, and X-ray returned without red flags. But when I nearly passed out while vacuuming the living room carpet, I took it as a warning to stop everything and practice rest, adoration, and worship, exorcising fear hiding deep underneath my calm, collected exterior. Thankfully, that early anxiety revealed fault lines in my faith; the places where trust was being misplaced. But it turns out, anxiety wasn't a completely accurate diagnosis.

As I awaited a phone call from the NHS (National Health Service) detailing time and date for the CT scan, the coronavirus pandemic began slowly invading Great Britain, making everything familiar, strange, and suspect. Daily news feeds blared with statistics on the unwell and dying in China, Italy, and Spain. Projections based on their horror informed preparations for an imminent battle. Three weeks behind Italy in terms of statistics, the virus would claim lives in England by the tens of thousands. Editing chapters themed around uncertainty while facing my own health crisis amid a pandemic, the serendipity seemed almost laughable. The words I wrote months earlier were being put to the test.

Facing imminent lockdown in London, the knee-jerk reaction to uncertainty among vast numbers of people manifested in hoarding. Pasta, tomato sauce, eggs, and toilet paper, normally taken for granted, appreciated overnight into valuable assets. Public transportation transmuted into a hazard, making a commute high-risk for contracting the virus. English cultural lifelines for cultivating community—pubs, parks, cafes, and theaters—changed into places of negative consequence.

When will we return to life as usual? How will global uncertainty disturb our mental health? Our livelihood? And future economy? What is God doing while the world is being shaken? These are familiar questions most of us asked during the early days of self-isolating and quarantine. And I was asking even more intimate questions while navigating a personal race with time as pain on my right side increased. I needed to be scheduled for a CT before all clinics closed and medical professionals were focused solely on Covid-19.

While waiting, routine blood work, X-rays, and meds were ordered to be filled at the least desirable place during an outbreak of a life-threatening virus: a busy hospital. Rain pouring down, I boarded a nearly empty train, massaging a swollen left leg while sitting down, keeping gloved hands away from seat cushions and metal bars, heart racing and breathless after the walk to the train station from my house. Disembarking at Paddington station, I quickly lost my bearings as I discovered a familiar landscape altered by cranes, blockades, and men wearing neon yellow vests and hard hats.

Holding an umbrella in one hand and phone in the other, jeans became rain-soaked along with my face as tears blurred the screen displaying the map leading to St. Mary's Hospital pharmacy. Feeling small, alone, and afraid underneath giant skyscrapers, I asked the closest yellow vest standing nearby, "Can you tell me how to get to the pharmacy through this maze of construction?" He smiles, points, and leads me in the right direction.

Tiny holes in an umbrella are insignificant when rain is spitting from the sky, but in a downpour, that hole makes an umbrella worthless for staying dry. In the same way, when we experience hardship, our faith provides a shield of protection from the enemy. We can become soaked by difficulty and experience God's love as a life raft keeping peace afloat. Adversity reveals where we have holes in our faith, where we have found comfort and security in the wrong things. We don't like it, but adversity draws us deeper into hope, highlighting our desperate need of him. It takes courage and trust in the unseen to press on during a life-threatening storm.

As I look back on that harrowing journey to the hospital, two things stand out to me: fear gains a stronghold when we become self-focused, and extending generosity amid uncertainty diffuses the power of fear to gain a stronghold.

In the hospital waiting room, I watched a young man on a break from work give up his place in line to have blood taken. There were too many people ahead of him and not enough time. I could've suggested exchanging places, but I was too self-absorbed. And that revelation made me want to be a better person. A person who is generous and outward-focused despite circumstances. I came home, messaged my neighbors, and left groceries on front stoops a few days later.

It was the kindness on the faces of a construction worker, phlebotomist, hospital employee, and stranger—making eye contact, smiling, slowing down to listen, and offering instruction—that calmed my anxiety that day. I want to be characterized as faithful, not fearful. Don't you?

As an early adapter and news junkie, my H implemented a *work from home* strategy among his staff before it became mandatory from the government. Our family room turned into his daytime office and sanctuary, meetings with colleagues and Sunday sermons were delivered virtually. And I continued a normal daily rhythm of working from home too.

In a matter of days, full waiting rooms of patients turned into empty concrete caverns with rows of unused vinyl chairs. From holding a number among rain-soaked patients to being the only person in a sterile room illuminated by fluorescent lights. Instead of delivering a sermon on Sunday morning, H accompanied me in an Uber to St. Mary's Hospital for a scan of my vital organs. One week later, I received a phone call from my doctor asking to meet at another clinic. Our neighborhood practice was already converted into a Covid intake.

"You can bring someone with you if you want to," she said before hanging up.

H canceled Zoom calls and together we learned that a tumor was identified in the soft tissue near my kidney, the exact place where I was experiencing pain. A biopsy was the next step, but the doctor expressed concern about scheduling. All the clinics were closing, making room for more Londoners identified as positive for the virus. Conversing in the hallway before leaving the clinic, my phone began vibrating in my coat pocket. It was the same person from St. Mary's I spoke to earlier, determined to get me on the books for the CT. He reported, "I have you scheduled for a biopsy next Friday."

For the week preceding the biopsy procedure, the spiritual practices I share with you in each chapter became daily rhythms, keeping my heart and mind at peace. Fear has no place to land when we are being held by love and belonging. And I knew I belonged to the Good Shepherd as I was wheeled into a cold, stark room holding medical equipment and radiographers. Once blue dye was inserted through a vein in my body for a second CT, the doctor overseeing the procedure came out of the viewing room, bent down on one knee, and said, "We found some things we didn't expect to see. Are you experiencing any swelling in your left leg? Or having trouble breathing?"

It turns out my symptoms were related after all. Not only was I a bit anxious, the tumor was pressing on vital organs and hindering blood flow. The CT revealed blood clots in both legs, chest, and lungs. Blood thinner was ordered, along with an overnight stay in the hospital for close monitoring, just as the coronavirus was ramping up in the city, making everyone anxious.

But there is more I want you to know. Because I believe in the power of prayer to heal and transform, and experience vulnerability as strength not weakness, as soon as I found out about the tumor, I shared the news publicly on social media. The communion of the saints is a beautiful thing to behold, especially in the wake of sobering news.

For nine hours straight, hundreds of messages, emails, and texts filled my inboxes with prayers, Scripture verses, and worship songs, keeping mind and heart in a peaceful repose. Pain was minimal as the prayers of the people saturated my senses and sinews. I wasn't alone in a hospital bed among strangers, I was being loved, comforted, and cared for by the sheep of the Good Shepherd around the globe. Don't keep your scary uncertainties to yourself. The quickest way to squelch fear is to tell someone about it.

As I await next steps for what doctors finally identified as sarcoma cancer growing in my body, watch daily news reports, the numbers of suffering people escalate; somehow our shared uncertainties make the unknown less scary for me. *I love you, you are not alone,* and *I am enough* are messages God has been communicating for thousands of years. Perhaps it is our in our shared lament that we are empowered to surpass circumstances, believe in hope, and trust that his Fatherly affections are certain. That's the beauty of redemption.

Practice Creative Captures That Conjure Intimacy with Christ

Note: These photography exercises can be adapted to a smartphone by using apps, filters, and editing programs.

Chapter One: Foundations

Find an image that is foundational to your roots; a picture that is a metaphor for who you are at the core. It can be a place, a thing, your mug at a young age. What is it about the image that draws you to it? Reframe what you see by being known by God. What deeper truth is God revealing than you first assumed on the surface? What does the image say about the foundations God has been laying for your one precious life? In community: Share your images and one new thing about yourself on Instagram with the hashtag #searchingforcertainty.

Chapter Two: Depth of Field

Practice using depth of field, making the object in the foreground clear and close, and the object in the background blurry and far away, and vice versa. Is there anything new you noticed? How does the contrast inform your capture? How does the image illustrate God's nearness or distance in your circumstances? What does the blur represent in your current situation? What are you not seeing with clarity right now? How might what you can see right in front of you bring revelation to what feels distant and out of reach? In community: Share your photo using the hashtag #searchingforcertainty. Tell us what you learned and how the image translates for you.

Chapter Three: Still Images

Still life exists within the moving pieces of your life. Capture stills in the rooms of your home or in the surrounding neighborhood. How does each detail in what you capture tell the story of your everyday, ordinary life? What would you like to remove from the photo? Why? What do you notice about the capture that you didn't see at first glance? What about the picture do you like and long to share? Tell us about the backstory behind the still image(s) in community with the hashtag #searchingforcertainty.

Chapter Four: Perspective

We often create unreasonably high standards for ourselves. In this exercise, we'll practice self-compassion. Take a selfie. What is one thing you see that you love? What are the mental edits on repeat in your head? What are you telling yourself when you look at your mug? How does being known and loved by God inform the way you see yourself? What would he say about the way you talk to yourself? In community: Share an unedited photo of yourself or something that reminds you of being loved and known for who you are, not what you do, using the hashtag #searchingforcertainty.

Chapter Five: Noise

A simple walk outdoors can calm unrest raging in your heart when uncertainty hits. Take a photo of a path or place you enjoy because of its calming effect. Snap a second photo of the same scene using a high ISO setting on your camera or a grainy filter on your phone (with a smartphone, this may require an app). What does the distortion do to the picture? How is the "noise" affecting clarity in the image? How is what you see in the photo a metaphor for discerning truth from falsity? How might busyness be distorting the way you view yourself and the world? In community: Share both photos using the hashtag #searchingforcertainty and tell us about the place you chose to photograph.

Chapter Six: Candids

Practice taking candids—those unplanned, unposed moments when life happens where you live. What surprises you about what you capture? How are you editing joy with fear? Capture a day in your life with candids. In community: Using the hashtag #searchingforcertainty, share three photos: morning, afternoon, and evening. Tell us what you love and what you wish you could change. What stands out to you as you recount the day? Where do you notice God afoot in your everyday moments? What are you thankful for as you look back?

Chapter Seven: Overexposure

Being overexposed can be a vulnerable posture. In this exercise, let's practice overexposing a capture by making adjustments on your camera or using an editing program to increase light. How does light enhance or detract from how you see things? What does the light expose? What does the light protect? Ask yourself those same questions personally, using a capital *L* for Light, meaning God. Share your overexposures and what you discover on Instagram with the hashtag #searchingforcertainty.

Chapter Eight: Polaroids

Let's practice beholding beauty through the lens in the same way God built the temple documenting particularities. For example, snap the veins of a leaf hanging from a tree, slanted light transforming colors in nature, a raindrop hanging from a stem, a bee surveying nectar in a flower, shadows on the walls of your house— beautiful, everyday signs of being shadowed by God's hand in your world. How does beauty change the atmosphere of your soul? How does beauty create calm for your uncertainty? What is the message God is sending through beautiful things? In community: Encourage others with your photos and thoughts by sharing the beauty you captured using the hashtag #searchingforcertainty.

Chapter Nine: Chiaroscuro

Shadows create mystery and mood aesthetically. In this exercise, let's practice chiaroscuro by capturing light and shadows when the sun is coming up or just going down in your part of the world. What mood does a shadow add to the scene you are capturing? Photograph in color and then edit to black and white. How does the change inform the certainty you first assumed in the composition of your photograph? What do shadows add to your photograph? In community: Share one photo each during sunrise and sunset, capturing shadows. Tell us about your experience using the hashtag #searchingforcertainty.

Chapter Ten: Black and White

Take black-and-white photos of the things around your house or in your neighborhood. How does the stark contrast inform your story? Name your collection of photographs with future generations in mind. What stories might the images tell your future self? How do they reflect being named by God? How do you hope future generations will name your life? In community: Share this exercise in image and words using the hashtag #searchingforcertainty.

Chapter Eleven: Bokeh

Use bokeh to make a pleasing aesthetic in your capture. Blur the background just enough that the object of focus is surrounded by a soft haze of light. Metaphorically, what does the blur in the background represent for you? What are the specifics in the foreground telling you? Are they creating wonder and gratitude? How is the blur of uncertainty in the photo (and life!) creating a pleasing composition? In community: Tell us about the image and answer the questions using the hashtag #searchingforcertainty on social media platforms.

Chapter Twelve: Sequence of Proofs

Photos, when linked together over time, give hints to how we are made and how we are called to glorify Christ. Create a sequence of proofs from the past or recent history that illustrate God's love in your life. Cull from galleries, files, and boxes of photos, ten images that tell a story of being loved and deeply known by the Creator. What details in the photos uniquely characterize intimacy in your relationship with God. In community: Share your images and, if you are brave, some of the details in the photos that tell us more about how God made you. When did he rescue, protect, comfort, and extend generosity and kindness? Let's glorify him through images and words using the hashtag #searchingforcertainty!

Acknowledgments

Dad, thanks for telling your story and allowing me to share it in the pages of this book. Our email conversations have been a gift of redemption.

Mom, even though we haven't talked in more than twenty years, I'm thankful that you raised me to love beauty, express creativity, and be resilient despite adversity. Our shared struggles in the early years made me who I am today.

Aunt Paula, your belief in me at every stage and age of life has been a rudder. Thank you for being the steady voice of love during the unsteady years growing up, and my memory now when I forget details.

H, thank you for being my rock of calm in the storms of life and the voice of truth when I doubt. Our family lives at peace because you are steadfast, safe, and secure in Christ's love.

Dea Moore, though your name is not mentioned in a chapter, your presence was felt on nearly every page. Your unceasing love, prayers, support, and encouragement have been an anchor in rough times and in seasons of calm. Thank you for being my person.

Michael and Avril Denton, your generosity is a gift always treasured. Thank you for providing constancy and security for me at Long House and in London. Long writing days don't feel so long in your comfy home.

Patreon community, thank you for providing a safe place to try new things and receive early feedback on content and ideas. Your support has been invaluable and deeply appreciated.

Terry Walling, thank for being my coach for over a decade. Your belief in me cultivated bravery for stepping into uncertain vocational waters. I'm confident I wouldn't be an author without your influence.

Sabbath Society and blog community, thank you for opening and responding to the pieces of writing I publish and send to your inboxes. Your voices shape and inform everything I write. Trusting me with your intimate stories makes me a richer writer. I'm grateful to have you in my corner.

Social media friends turned global prayer warriors: Wow! Did I hit the jackpot when our paths converged! Thank you for unceasing devotion to intercede on my behalf. Your words have been a comfort, compass, and conviction. I'm deeply indebted. You know who you are.

Writing comrades—thanks to Jennifer Dukes Lee who always provides insight and practical help early in the writing process. Your friendship is a treasure. For Ann Kroeker, who generously persevered during the conception stages, culling the felt need and brainstorming titles for months—your coaching gifts are priceless. Thanks to Megan Willome for your stellar poetry critiques on the poems I included. A big thank-you to Christie Purifoy, Kimberly Coyle, Kristin Schell, Sara Hagerty, and Sally Clarkson for encouragement, support, and practical advice. And Emily Freeman, your written and spoken words have been a teacher, mentor, and kindred friend for many years. Thank you for shaping my faith and writing the foreword. I'm honored and humbled by your yes.

To my agent, Janet Grant, thank you for being my advocate. Your experience and wisdom made this book a reality. To my editor, Jeff Braun, and the Bethany House team, thank you for believing in the message of *Searching for Certainty*, trusting me, and saying *yes!* in a million little ways.

Notes

Chapter 1 Reframing Uncertainty

1. "The State of Mental Health in America 2019," Mental Health America, https://www.mhanational.org/issues/state-mental-health-america.

2. Alex Williams, "How Anxiety Became Society's Prevalent Condition," *The Independent*, June 17, 2017, https://www.independent.co.uk/news/long_reads/anxiety-prozac-nation-depression-mental-health-disorder-america-panic-usa-memoirs-self-help-book-a7785351.html.

Chapter 3 Shhh! Be Still

1. Esther de Waal, *The Celtic Way of Prayer* (London: Canterbury Press, 2010), 211.

2. Catherine Hommes, "Peregrinatio, Pilgrimage Celtic Style," *Culture Honey*, October 1, 2015, http://www.culturehoney.com/peregrinatio-pilgrimage-celtic-style/.

3. Luci Shaw, *Breath for the Bones* (Nashville: Thomas Nelson, 2007), Loc 1860.

Chapter 4 Breaking Habits

1. Charles Duhigg, *The Power of Habit* (New York: Random House, 2012), 20.

2. Duhigg, *The Power of Habit*, 78.

3. Duhigg, *The Power of Habit*, 89.

Chapter 5 Help Me Decide

1. Kristin Schell, *The Turquoise Table: Finding Community and Connection in Your Own Front Yard* (Nashville: Thomas Nelson, 2017).

2. Emily P. Freeman, *The Next Right Thing: A Simple, Soulful Practice for Making Life Decisions* (Grand Rapids, MI: Revell, 2019), 17.

3. Eugene Peterson, *As Kingfishers Catch Fire* (Colorado Springs: Waterbrook, 2017), 223.

Chapter 7 Winning or Whining?

1. Brennan Manning, *Ruthless Trust: The Ragamuffin's Path to God* (New York: Harper Collins, 2000), 37.

2. Ana Swanson, "What really drives you crazy about waiting in line (it actually isn't the wait at all)," *Washington Post*, November 27, 2015, https://www.washingtonpost.com/news/wonk/wp/2015/11/27/what-you-hate-about-waiting-in-line-isnt-the-wait-at-all/.

3. Esther de Waal, *The Celtic Way of Prayer: The Recovery of the Religious Imagination* (London: Canterbury Press, 2010), Loc 94.

Chapter 8 Beholding Beauty for the Big Picture

1. Rosalind Wiseman, *Masterminds and Wingmen* (New York: Harmony Books, 2013), 18.

2. John O'Donohue, *Divine Beauty* (London: Bantam Books, 2003), 226.

3. Emily P. Freeman, "Before Helpless Turns into Hopeless," https://emilypfreeman.com/before-helpless-turns-to-hopeless/.

4. Eugene Peterson, *As Kingfishers Catch Fire*, 89.

Chapter 9 Rest When Shadowed by Worry

1. Dorothy Day, *The Reckless Way of Love* (Walden, NY: Plough Publishing, 2017), Loc 624.

2. Ann Voskamp, *The Greatest Gift* (Carol Stream, IL: Tyndale Publishers, 2013), 233.

3. Esther de Waal, *The Celtic Way of Prayer* (London: Canterbury Press, 2010), Loc 243.

4. Irving Schattner, "Why Do We Worry So Much?" *Psych Central*, October 8, 2018, https://psychcentral.com/lib/why-do-we-worry-so-much/.

5. Emily P. Freeman, "Let's Share What we Learned this Summer," https://emilypfreeman.com/lets-share-learned-summer-2017/.

6. Luci Shaw, *Breath for the Bones* (Nashville: Thomas Nelson, 2007), Loc 2141.

Chapter 10 Named and Known

1. Christie Purifoy, *Roots and Sky* (Grand Rapids, MI: Revell, 2016).

2. John Mark Comer, *God Has a Name* (Grand Rapids, MI: Zondervan, 2017), Loc 3351.

3. John Mark Comer, *God Has a Name* (Grand Rapids, MI: Zondervan, 2017), Loc 886.

4. Patty Onderko, "The Benefits of Experiencing a Wider Range of Emotions," *Success*, December 13, 2017, https://www.success.com/the-benefits-of-experiencing-a-wider-range-of-emotions/.

5. Angela Lee Duckworth, "Grit: The Power of Passion and Perseverance," TED Talk, April 2013, https://www.ted.com/talks/angela_lee_duckworth_grit_the_power_of_passion_and_perseverance?language=en.

Chapter 11 Gratitude Brings Focus to the Blur of Uncertainty

1. Frederick Buechner, *The Faces of Jesus* (Brewster, MA: Paraclete, 1974, 2006), 95.

2. C.S. Lewis, *The Screwtape Letters* (New York: Macmillan, 1943), 44.

Shelly Miller is a veteran ministry leader and sought-after spiritual mentor and leadership coach. She is the author of *Rhythms of Rest: Finding the Spirit of Sabbath in a Busy World* and leads the Sabbath Society, an online global community that practices weekly rest as reality. She is described as a poet with an acute taste for authentic honesty, and a storyteller and avid photographer who helps people think about and see life differently. Making their home in London, England, Shelly and her husband, H, are the proud parents of two adult children.

Engage with Shelly's writing, coaching, and life in London on the following platforms:

Instagram	@shellymillerwriter
Facebook	@shellymillerwriter
Website	shellymillerwriter.com
Patreon	Patreon.com/ShellyMiller

More from Shelly Miller

With warmth and encouragement, this book shows how even busy people can find a rhythm of rest in their lives—whether for an hour, a morning, or a whole day. Learn simple, practical ways to rest, and even how meals and times with loved ones can be Sabbath experiences. Rest is a gift from God, one that will refresh you mentally, physically, and spiritually.

Rhythms of Rest

BETHANYHOUSE

Stay up to date on your favorite books and authors with our free e-newsletters. Sign up today at bethanyhouse.com.

 facebook.com/BHPnonfiction

 @bethany_house

@bethany_house_nonfiction